D1474784

SOCIALIZATION AND EDUCATION

**Recent Titles in
Contributions to the Study of Education**

SOCIALIZATION AND EDUCATION

Essays in Conceptual Criticism

Wolfgang Brezinka

Translated by James Stuart Brice

Contributions to the Study of Education, *Number 63*

GREENWOOD PRESS
Westport, Connecticut • London

Library of Congress Cataloging-in-Publication Data

Brezinka, Wolfgang.
    Socialization and education : essays in conceptual criticism /
Wolfgang Brezinka ; translated by James Stuart Brice.
        p. cm.—(Contributions to the study of education, ISSN
0196–707X ; no. 63)
    Includes bibliographical references and indexes.
    ISBN 0–313–29258–2 (alk. paper)
    1. Education—Social aspects—Philosophy. 2. Socialization.
I. Title. II. Series.
    LC192.4.B74 1994
    370.19—dc20   93–47087

British Library Cataloguing in Publication Data is available.

Library of Congress Catalog Card Number: 93–47087
ISBN: 0–313–29258–2
ISSN: 0196–707X

First published in 1994

Greenwood Press, 88 Post Road West, Westport, CT 06881
An imprint of Greenwood Publishing Group, Inc.

Printed in the United States of America

The paper used in this book complies with the
Permanent Paper Standard issued by the National
Information Standards Organization (Z39.48–1984).

10 9 8 7 6 5 4 3 2 1

Copyright Acknowledgment

Originally published as "Sozialisation und Erziehung,"
"'Modelle' in Erziehungstheorien," and "Konflikterziehung,"
pages 192–320, in *Aufklärung über Erziehungstheorien:
Beiträge zur Kritik der Pädagogik* by Ernst Reinhardt Verlag,
Munich, Basel, 1989.

Contents

Preface

> One can think about a subject only insofar
> as one has distinct concepts of it; where
> these cease, ignorance begins.
>
> CHRISTOPH MARTIN WIELAND
> 1797 (1984: 471).

There is a lack of clearly defined concepts in the social sciences. Social scientists are all too prone to adopting the latest fashionable words and slogans. The prevailing linguistic unclarity is a consequence of unclear thinking and itself tends to promote unclear thinking. But if we do not recognize vague and ambiguous concepts, statements and statement systems for what they are, they will continue to retard the process of acquiring social scientific knowledge. Therefore linguistic and conceptual analysis is among the necessary prerequisites for unmasking pseudo-knowledge and achieving real knowledge.

This book carefully examines three terms which in the last few decades have become widespread in the social sciences. The greatest amount of attention will be devoted to the term "*socialization.*" Authors of many texts on this topic fail to state precisely what they intend it to mean. Often "socialization" is confused with "education" and "education" with "socialization." Though a fashionable word, it is one which, instead of facilitating, tends to interfere with precise thinking. Its inflationary use is a symptom of conceptual confusion, which prevails as much in psychological and sociological theories of the emergence of personality as in educational theories dealing with actions intended to guide this process.

The conceptual confusion is similarly great with the use of the fashionable word "*model.*" The second chapter is devoted to this term. The third investigates the slogan "*conflict education*" and its theoretical background. I hope that my criticism of vague and misleading ideas can make a contribution to raising the standards of concept formation in the social sciences in general and in educational theories in particular. This would be an important step toward facilitating communication and cooperative work on educational theories.

This book supplements my *Basic Concepts of Educational Science*, published in 1994 by the University Press of America, Lanham, MD/New York/ London. The epistemological foundations of my conceptual analyses are explained in *Philosophy of Educational Knowledge* (Dordrecht/Boston/London 1992: Kluwer Academic Publishers).

I wish to thank James Stuart Brice for his excellent translation. He has succeeded in conveying the precise nuances of the original text in an easily readable and idiomatic style. I have personally corrected the English text and given it my approval.

I gratefully dedicate this book to my friend Leopold Rosenmayr, professor of sociology at the University of Vienna. For thirty-five years we have been bound together through the exchange of critical ideas. The chapter "Socialization and Education" is, furthermore, based on a lecture I gave at his invitation on 9 June 1988 at the Institute for Sociology of the University of Vienna.

SOCIALIZATION
AND
EDUCATION

1

Socialization and Education

Since the mid-twentieth century the word "socialization" has been used increasingly in the social sciences.[1] Between 1950 and 1960 "socialization" became a fashionable name for the process by which the social personality comes into existence and the influence which socio-cultural conditions have on this process. The becoming of personality is, however, an extremely complex process, one involving numerous factors, both known and unknown. While great strides have been made in understanding their nature and interaction, much remains to be learned or never will be. In this research area there has been and continues to be great scope for supposition, competing interpretations based on opposing images of man and the choice of various subissues and terminologies. The term "socialization" has gone through a variety of shifts in meaning over the years, as the theoretical foundations of different socialization theories have been criticized and revised, but its popularity continues unabated.

CONCEPTUAL CONFUSION ABOUT "SOCIALIZATION"

Despite its absorption into the vocabularies of different fields of study in various social sciences, including psychology, sociology, anthropology, ethology, pedagogics,[2] social work and political science, and despite the numerous texts devoted to it, the meaning of "socialization" remains unclear. On the one hand, it refers to an inner process through which people become "social." On the other, to external processes in people's environments through which they are "made social." Included among these external processes is education. Finally, the word can additionally refer to the whole constellation of internal and external processes leading to the emergence (coming into existence) of the "social" or "socialized" personality, or the personality "capable of social action."

Since its introduction, the word "socialization" has been one of the vaguest terms in the vocabulary of the social sciences. This vagueness has not prevented the creation of a great number of compound and derivative terms, giving the impression of a basic scientific concept, one so clear and fruitful that "socialization" terminology could be used in theory formulation.

In the literature we read of "family," "parental," "school," "professional," "political" and "religious" socialization; of "cognitive," "linguistic," "emotional," "motivational," "moral," "musical," "sexual" and "gender-specific" socialization; of "primary," "secondary" and "tertiary" socialization; of "childhood" and "adult" socialization; of "socialization types," "socialization styles," "socialization methods," "socialization techniques" and "socialization practices"; of "socialization facilities," "socialization instances," "socialization agencies," "socialization institutions," "socialization influences," "socialization milieus"; of "socialization environments," "socialization fields" and "socialization systems"; of "socialization programs," "socialization offerings," "socialization achievements," "socialization attempts," "socialization assistance," "socialization training," "socialization experiences," "socialization needs" and "socialization efforts"; of "socialization effects," "socialization results," "socialization successes," "socialization deficits," and "socialization deprivation"; of "socializedness,"[3] "under-socialization," "over-socialization" and "resocialization"; of "socialization patterns," "socialization aims," "socialization tasks" and "socialization contents"; of "socializands," "socializees," "persons to be socialized," "objects of socialization" and "persons handicapped by socialization"; of "socializers," "bearers of socialization," "socialization personnel," "agents of socialization" and "socialization experts" as "specialists in steering the socialization process";[4] of "socializing interaction," of the "role of socializer," the "power" and "monopoly of socializers."

We also read of "successful" and "unsuccessful," of "fortunate" and "unfortunate," "disturbed" and "incorrectly performed," of "satisfactory," "deviant" and "deficient," of "affirmative" and "emancipatory," of "symmetrical" and "asymmetrical" socialization. We encounter the action words "to socialize" and "to resocialize"; the attribute words "socializing," "socialization-effective," "socialized" and "unsocializable," "correctly" socialized and "incorrectly" socialized. Some even speak of "need for socialization,"[5] of "socialization policy"[6] and "socialization law":[7] many additional examples could also be listed.[8] We even come across such odd expressions as "self-socialization"[9] and "socialization engineer."[10]

All these terms stem from texts which are regarded as contributions to "socialization research," "socialization theory" or "socialization science."[11] Perceptive scholars naturally know quite well that in this area there is still a great need for precise concepts and theories. Socialization rhetoric has, however, already made such a great impression on the credulous public that "knowledge of socialization theory" must be demonstrated in examinations for teaching positions,[12] and students in secondary schools are urged to study the "interdependence of development and socialization."[13]

Socialization vocabulary has also been very quickly absorbed into popular intellectual jargon. Thus far beyond academically educated social circles it has helped make contemporary confusion in thinking and speaking about educational questions greater than ever before. In Germany this confusion is even promoted politically. The 1975 "Second Family Report of the Federal Minister for Youth, Family and Health" abounds with confusing statements regarding the relationship between education and socialization. Responsible for this report was an expert committee under the chairmanship of well-known sociologist Friedhelm Neidhardt. The committee expressly "preferred speaking of *socialization* instead of education and of socialization aims instead of educational aims."[14] Since the authors at the same time held fast to the current sense of "socialization" as a name for learning processes, the text suffered from great conceptual confusion.

Unfortunately, however, this is no isolated case. Rather, on closely analyzing the relevant social science texts one finds that of the various existing concepts of socialization the vaguest is used the most frequently. It has roughly the following contents: an undifferentiated sum of the person's growth, development and learning, influencing, forming and educating, being influenced, being formed and being educated. The word is used as a collective name for one of the most complex things imaginable: *for the genesis and change of the human personality over the entire lifespan from birth to death and for all socio-cultural conditions upon which this is dependent, as well as for the sum of all actions through which, depending on their differing aims, people attempt to influence it.*[15]

One cannot formulate even a simple hypothesis on the basis of such a vague concept, let alone a scientific theory. Since the meaning of the root word "socialization" is unclear, the entire manifold socialization terminology based on it has degenerated into ambiguous slogans. Instead of furthering our knowledge of the world, it makes orientation more difficult, because it confuses things which should be clearly differentiated. The pervasive conceptual ambiguity in the problem area of "socialization" detracts from clear thinking precisely where the central substantive matter of both individual and societal life ought to be clarified.

How can this unfortunate situation be ameliorated? What can we do in order to overcome conceptual confusion? Critical thinkers could refuse to employ the term "socialization." This would, however, not prevent it from continuing to be widely used, for it is the bearer of meanings which, despite all their inadequacies, are considered important and worthy of being communicated. Therefore it would not help much to denigrate the word "socialization" without having first examined the possible scientific value of its various senses. Rather, the conceptual field to which it belongs must be clarified and the objects to which it refers examined. This will make clear whether there is a sense of the word "socialization" which could be scientifically fruitful and thus deserves to be precisely defined. Only if we can formulate an unambiguous and sufficiently exact concept of socialization, one fitting into a system of other clear and fruitful concepts, will it be worthwhile to continue using the word "socialization": as a name for this precisely defined concept and nothing else.

ETYMOLOGICAL ANALYSIS OF THE WORD "SOCIALIZATION"

The authors who introduced this social scientific technical term—what were they referring to? What meanings were intended by its users? In order to answer these questions, examples of linguistic usage must be collected, examined and compared. Since the word "socialization" contains the stem "social," a glance at its meanings is appropriate.

Meanings of the Word "Social"

The word "social" goes back to the Latin "socialis," related to "socius" and "societas." The substantive "socius" means: comrade, participant; "societas" means: society, community, cooperative, connection to others. The adjective "socialis" means: belonging to comrades, sociable, social, concerning society.[16] The original meaning of the Indogermanic root "*seq*" (Latin: sequi, to follow, accompany) is: to be together, to be with. English has also drawn on the French "social" and "socialise," themselves derived from Latin.[17]

Many senses are associated with the English word "*so-*

cial,"[18] from which the words "socialization" and "to socialize" have been formed. As a term belonging to the study of society it dates back at least to the nineteenth century, although the various meanings have changed over time. In social science texts it refers, on the one hand, to "any behaviour or attitude that is influenced by past or present experience of the behaviour of other people (direct or indirect), or that is oriented (consciously or unconsciously) toward other people," and, on the other hand, to every "action directed in some sense toward the welfare of others—and usually toward the welfare either of a whole society or its less privileged members."[19]

The word "*sozial*" was first adopted into German toward the end of the eighteenth century; however, it became widespread only after the mid-nineteenth century.[20] Subsequently it soon became one of the most ambiguous words in the German language. The most commonly encountered meanings are the following:[21]

1. Living together, community, relevant to human (or animal) society, societal. Antonyms are "individual" (relevant to the individual) and "personal" (relevant to people as persons).

2. Leading a social life as an essential attribute of man ("homo sociale animal") and animals. Antonym: "solitary."

3. Relevant to several persons (or animals), collective.

4. Interpersonal, relevant to the relations between persons. Antonym: "psychic," "intra-personal."

5. Relevant to the situation, position or economic circumstances of a person (or of several persons) in society (or in a group).

6. Relevant to qualities (psychic dispositions) or modes of behavior (or behavior taken as a whole) which persons possess who, with respect to accepted norms, are recognized as completely adequate members of their group. Antonyms are "unsocial," "socially harmful," "hostile to society," "asocial," "antisocial."

7. Having an attraction to others, loving company, val-

uing other people's company, sociable. Antonym: "individualistic."

8. Promoting community, useful to the community, obligated to the community, showing regard for others; relevant to the common good, i.e., the good of fellow human beings, the community and society as a whole. Antonyms: "egoistic," "group-centric," "class-centric."

9. Relevant to the theory of socialism, socialistic societal critique, the realization of socialistic ideals; socialistic.

10. Relevant to the advancement of lower social classes, economically weak and dependent groups of persons; relevant to protecting the interests of workers and the improvement of their condition.

11. Charitable, benevolent, helpful; protective of those in need of protection, helpful to the suffering.

This overview is by no means complete. It does, however, suffice to indicate the rich variety of descriptive, evaluative and normative meanings associated with the word "social,"[22] from which the words "socialization" and "to socialize" have been formed.

This rich variety is itself a source of countless misunderstandings. Therefore attempts have been made for quite some time to unburden the word "social" of meanings, at least in scientific language, by partially replacing it with other less ambiguous and affective words.[23]

The ambiguity of the word "social" also burdens the derived word "socialization." A particular factor is that "social" has not only value-neutral descriptive senses such as "related to fellow human beings," "inter-personal" or "relevant to society," but also evaluative senses such as "relevant to public welfare," "advancing the community," "socialistic" or "humanitarian." Besides descriptive and evaluative (denotative) senses, "socialization" also has emotion-arousing overtones and a relatively large connotative "sphere," i.e., an "associatively aroused surrounding field of obscurely formed conceptions which do not move into the center of consciousness,"[24] both of which tend to evoke pre-rational intuitive responses. While one individual may feel that "socialization" means something good, valuable or positive, another may see it as threatening, collectivistic or socialistic, as something which can reduce personal freedom and self-responsibility. Among the reasons for this is that the word "socialization" was first employed in the political-economic sense before it was adopted into the vocabularies of sociology, psychology and pedagogics.

Political-Economic Meanings of "Socialization"

In order to make clear that the political-economic meanings of the term "socialization" refer to *actions* and not to mere courses of events or processes which occur without any aim, it is best to start with the verb "to socialize." It has two main political-economic senses in English: to "place under government or group ownership or control" (also referred to as nationalization), and to "convert or adapt to the needs of society."

Socialization as the Deprivatization of Economic Goods

"To socialize" economic goods (especially means of production) can mean one of two things: transferring them from private to community ownership or the introduction of "limitations on disposal which are imposed on owners, whereby both forms are alleged to be either set up in the interest of society as a whole or, after having been set up, permanently serving this interest."[25]

In a narrower sense of the word only transfer to community ownership is intended. Such deprivatization can occur through nationalization, communalization or the formation of public corporations to replace private ones. "Nationalization" is thus only one, even if it is (besides "confiscation") the most popular sense of the word "to socialize."

"To socialize" (or "socialization") *refers in each case to a means of achieving specific purposes*. It is a component of an end-means relationship. Among the ends can be the carrying out of a division of income which for reasons of justice eliminates private income not based on work performance (income from capital); overcoming private (but also public) monopoly power or compensating for the negative effects of monopolies; carrying out general (macro-economic) planning in the sense of a socialistic planned economy. Depending on the circumstances, various different means are needed to achieve these ends.[26]

Introduction of a Socialistic Societal Order

In a broader sense one understands socialization[27] to mean "all the measures which further or introduce a socialistic societal and economic order."[28] As with deprivatization, measures of this sort are also actions directed at achieving aims or ends. They are means to ends.

The above comments make clear how ambiguous the word "socialization" is, even confined to a political-economy context. Therefore it was already recommended in the sixties "to reject this ambiguous expression, which has become a slogan and in each case to precisely designate the objective problem which one intends."[29] One should replace "socialization" with "more precise expressions, which in many cases could be done without great difficulty."[30] In fact, however, after sociologists took possession of the term just the opposite happened.

Sociological, Psychological and Pedagogical Meanings of "Socialization"

"Socialization" is a cognate of "social" and "society," and thus understandably of particular interest to sociologists. It is, however, not merely a matter of a single topic, but of several dealt with under the same name.

Group-Related Concepts of Socialization

When the term first came into use, it was employed in connection with the most general questions of sociology: "How do groups arise?" or "How is society possible?"[31] In this sense Simmel referred to "*the construction of a socie-tal unity out of individuals*" as achieved by "socialization" processes.[32]

Similarly, Oppenheimer used the word "socialization" as the "association" of *groups* through the creation of values, norms and institutions such as law, religion and customs.[33] Lochner also employed the term as a synonym for "the process of forming groups," "the formation of community," "the binding of persons to one another."[34] For Max Weber, to the contrary, the words "Vergesell-schaftung" (socialization) and "Vergemeinschaftung" refer to two types of "*social relationships*," whereby he understands "social relationships" as meaning "the behavior of a plurality of actors insofar as, in its meaningful content, the action of each takes account of that of the others and is oriented in these terms."[35]

These senses of the word "socialization" (and its synonyms) thus refer to processes involving groups, their creation and self-preservation. They are group-related concepts of socialization.

Person-Related Concepts of Socialization

In studying the creation and continued existence of groups one naturally comes across the question of how new generations acquire the personality qualities necessary for maintaining the cohesiveness of groups and for the fulfillment of their tasks. How do the "little barbarians,"[36] born immature but plastic, formable and capable of anything, become persons specifically endowed with precisely the abilities, knowledge, beliefs and desires which are most consistent with the life order of their society? Everyone comes "into the world raw,"[37] without culture and wild. "What tames our little ones?" "What civilizes the little wild creatures in our midst?"[38] How do their "civilization," "cultivation," "disciplining" and "moralization" proceed?

This theme is an old one and the above-cited expressions were already used by Kant.[39] As early as 1908, McDougall called "the moralization or socialization" of the individual by society the "fundamental problem of social psychology."[40] This usage refers not to the origin of groups, but to a person's "becoming social" in the framework of an already-present group, the creation of the "socialized subject" or the "socialized person."[41] The socialization concepts employed in this research area focus on processes through which *persons* change. They refer to the "becoming of the personality"[42] or, more problematically expressed, the "development,"[43] especially "social development,"[44] of the person. Only these *person-related* senses of the word "socialization" will be examined below.

One must thereby determine what sorts of concepts are used to explain the senses of this term. There is, in fact, an astonishing variety of such concepts. The greatest share can, however, be grouped in the following four conceptual classes:

1. The concepts poorest in content and most extensive are the "*becoming*," "*formation*," "*emergence*," "*creation*" or "*genesis of the personality*." In these cases "socialization" is understood as the "development of psychic structures on the basis of environmental conditions,"[45] the "genesis of the personality on the basis of societal conditions"[46] or "becoming a human subject" as a "*psychic process*."[47] Many authors limit this process to the becoming of the "social character" or the "social person."[48] In any event, "socialization" means here a process completed *in the person* of the one who is becoming: an intra-personal process.

2. "Socialization" is often described using the concepts of "*learning*," "social learning," "societally relevant learning," "taking on," "receiving," "acquiring," "assimilating," "absorbing," or "internalizing." In these cases as well, the reference is to a process which takes place *within the person* of the learner.

What is learned, the *learning content*, is designated with the following concepts: "*dispositions*" which make people "more or less able members of their society";[49] "socially relevant behavioral and experiential schemata";[50] "behavioral norms";[51] "social value orientations"; "social role expectations";[52] "social behavior which the group recognizes";[53] "the culture" of one's own group, "role prescriptions and role behavior," "habits, beliefs, attitudes, and motives";[54] "socio-cultural contents";[55] "behavioral qualifications" which are necessary in order "to be able to communicate with other members of society";[56] "norms and value systems";[57] "modes of behavior," "styles of thinking, feelings, knowledge, motivation and convictions";[58] and, finally, as the most comprehensive content: "humanness"[59] or "humanity."

Clearly the term "*social learning*" is used in two fundamentally different senses. In the first case the term "social" relates to the *contents* or the *results* of learning: to *psychic dispositions* relevant for community life—be it from the learner's viewpoint, that of society or from both viewpoints taken together. In the second case the word "social" relates to the *conditions* under which learning occurs or on which it depends: to *social partners* from whom people learn and/or *social interactions* through which or in which learning occurs.

3. "Socialization" is also explicated using concepts such as "*influencing*," "forming," "reforming," "moulding" or "imprinting the person";[60] "*social influence* on . . . personalities";[61] "transmission of behavioral dispositions";[62] "imparting of . . . value orientations, norms, action- and attitudinal patterns";[63] "influence on the activities" of an individual;[64] "induction of an individual into . . . a society";[65] or the "process by which society creates persons suitable to carry out its functional requirements."[66]

The bearers of these processes are influencing factors *outside the persons influenced*. The person is here the object of influence. "Socialization" in this sense is a societal, thus extra-personal process.

4. "Socialization" is described by many authors either in part or entirely with the following expressions: "*education*"; "child rearing";[67] "guiding," "caring for";[68] "instruction"; "training";[69] "efforts . . . to transmit and secure adherence to existing norms."[70] The spectrum of meanings extends in this case from "*making social*"[71] in general to

"education for consideration"[72] or "education in social thinking"[73] in particular.

This overview shows that the social-scientific term "socialization" is explicated by means of quite various concepts which are themselves more or less unclear. Depending on the concepts employed in explications, the word "socialization" has various meanings. However, many who use the term are unaware of its ambiguity. They think they are using a concept, when they are merely employing a name for various quite different things. Since there are no generally recognized rules for deciding when and where it should be used, misunderstandings are almost unavoidable among those who speak of "socialization."

These misunderstandings could to be sure be reduced if users would specify the sense in which *they* employ the term "socialization" and then hold consistently to this sense. However, characteristic of the existing conceptual confusion is that many authors do not stay with the sense they have themselves defined, but instead use the term "socialization" in other senses, even in the same text, and often without noticing this. *The ambiguous and inconsistent use of a central term shows that the entire system of ideas to which it belongs is unclear.* Conceptual inadequacies are always a sign of deficient theories, as is the case with socialization theory. This will be shown using texts by twenty-four representative authors.

Before beginning with these examples, I wish to make clear that while the conceptual confusion found in the problem area "socialization" does, to be sure, burden all sciences, it is especially serious in educational science, and thereby indirectly affects educators, who are influenced by it.

Lack of Clarity Concerning the Relationship Between Socialization and Education

The adoption of unclear socialization concepts by educational science has led to a relapse into a conceptual and theoretical confusion which, judging from the results of recent conceptual analytic studies,[74] one might be tempted to think had already been overcome. In particular, use of the term "socialization" has revived the old confused conceptions which sixty years ago were spread with such vague concepts as "*education as a social function*,"[75] "*functional education*"[76] or education as "adaptation" through "social assimilation."[77]

This confusion began with Durkheim, who as early as the beginning of our century defined *education as "a methodical socialization of the young generation*" which must create in each person "the social being."[78] How great the conceptual confusion has in the meantime become is apparent from a 1973 textbook on *General Educational Science* (Allgemeine Erziehungswissenschaft, Röhrs). The author of this text asserts that there are "no ultimately valid and rigid boundaries between socialization, enculturation and education, for in a pedagogically motivated field the one runs into the other"; "socialization is a process which accompanies becoming and being human, one which can at any time be transformed into education."[79]

In German pedagogics the redundant expression "education and Bildung" ("Bildung" is a synonym of "education"), which has even found its way into constitutions and school laws,[80] has long been symptomatic of a lack of conceptual clarity on the part of those who use it. Ever since "socialization" vocabulary became fashionable, numerous similarly inane combinations of the words "socialization" and "education" have been commonplace. We read of the "process of socialization and education,"[81] of "socializing, educating and formative functions and intentions,"[82] of the "socializing and educating task of the school system,"[83] etc. But we are not informed as to whether and how the meanings of these compound expressions differ. Is it merely a matter of two names for one concept? Or of two concepts? In the latter case their composite use would only be logically justified if they referred to two different objects, domains or topics on the same level of abstraction which formed two subclasses of a higher-level class or two species of a genus. This would presuppose that one had a single criterion for selection and that the senses of the two terms did not overlap.

In fact, however, there is no clarity about the relationship between "socialization" and "education," because authors employ these terms for quite different (and by and large imprecisely defined) concepts. In one case it is emphasized: "Socialization is not identical with education";[84] in another, that it is "in broad areas identical with education";[85] "the sharp distinction between socialization and education" has "hardly proved itself."[86] One group of writers asserts that "education" is "a subconcept of socialization";[87] education can be "understood as a sector of socialization";[88] "the traditional concept of education" is "included in the concept of socialization."[89] Some authors are of a contrary opinion: "The process of socialization represents only one side of education as a whole."[90] One even claims that "socialization" is "the *functional* aspect of education" and conversely, that "education" could be "paraphrased as the *intentional* part of socialization."[91]

This terminological confusion favors quite *different evaluations* of words and concepts, even *ideologically or politically motivated disputes* over the words "socialization" and "education" and their meanings. Roessler is of the opinion that the increasing use of the word "socialization" as a substitute for the words "education" and "Bildung" shows "a new understanding of education . . . in connection with a new understanding of the world and of man."[92] Bittner, to the contrary, believes that "the" socialization concept "tendentiously" blocks "the whole pedagogical task": it "radically" nullifies "the question of the person's individuality, self-sufficiency and self-responsibility."[93]

The foolishness of replacing the word "to educate" with the word "to socialize" has triggered a counter-movement for the "defense of education" as a word, concept and subject.[94] We are warned by one author about the "danger in the concept of socialization."[95] Another author is of a different opinion: dangerous or not—"the end of educa-

tion" is at any rate in view: it is "increasingly being replaced by socialization"—"even where education sup-
posedly still occurs."[96]

This controversy shows that a lack of clear concepts
has even led to misunderstandings severe enough to provide material for moral, ideological and political disputes.
Originally introduced as a technical scientific term intended to designate in an unprejudicial manner specific
(hypothetically assumed) psychic or social processes,
"socialization" has become a *slogan*, a "type of 'ultimate
category' with a comprehensive valence which crosses
over into the ideological."[97]

More often than a "value neutral descriptive concept of
socialization," one now encounters a "prescriptive concept of socialization weighted down by specific value conceptions."[98] We read of the "claim of the socializand to
socialization" and of society's "duty" to provide "socializing services."[99] One author maintains "that socialization
aims are the true center of interest in a theory of socialization" and "that we can really only develop a theory of
socialization once we have" agreed on "a binding societal
utopia."[100] "Socialization" is brought into a relationship
with a program for changing our "entire society": "If . . .
socialization processes are to be changed, society as a
whole must simultaneously be changed."[101]

Even in scientific discussion lack of conceptual clarity
has led to unnecessary polarization. Especially through
questions such as "education or socialization?"[102] and
"socialization or education?"[103] the impression is con-
veyed that it is a matter thereby of terminological alternatives between which one can and must choose. To the
contrary, it is more reasonable to think that *both* terms
can be useful, insofar as they stand for *different* concepts relating to different segments of the world. The
question is: which segments? Let us look at what representative texts have to say about this.

EXAMPLES OF USAGE IN ANGLO-AMERICAN SOCIALIZATION LITERATURE

Parsons

Talcott Parsons, writing in 1951, started from the premise that the term "socialization" was primarily related to "the process of child development." He used it, however, in reference to a particular type of learning process: the learning of "value-orientation patterns" or "the learning of *any* orientations of functional significance to the operation of a system of complementary role-expectations. In this sense, socialization, like learning, goes on throughout life."[104]

Parsons was among those most responsible for popularizing the term "socialization" in American sociology. His concept of socialization is part of a complicated role theory based conceptual system which cannot be presented in greater detail here. For our semantic analysis it suffices to state that he explained socialization as a *learning process* (I): as "the learning of social role-expectations," as the "acquisition of the requisite orientations for satisfactory functioning in a role," as "social learning," as "the internalization of certain patterns of value-orientation"[105] and as "the internalization of the culture of the society into which the child is born."[106]

Clearly we can only add to our understanding of learning processes if we investigate their underlying conditions. *However, confusion is spread if learning processes are terminologically confused with their (external or "social") conditions or subconditions.* Precisely this happens continually in the writings of Parsons and many other authors. Already the introduction of the term "socializing agent"[107] is incompatible with a definition of "socialization" as a learning process, if this agent is not a person who "learns socially" or "socializes" himself. What is actually intended is a person who "socializes" the learner or by whom the learner is "socialized." If one then speaks of "socialization mechanisms of reward-punishment," of "socialization by instruction" and of the "socializing agent" as a "teacher,"[108] the reference can no longer be to a learning process within the individual, but only to a *process of influencing* or even of *educational action* directed at the individual from without (II). The same holds if the school is referred to as an "agency of socialization"[109] "through which individual personalities are trained to be motivationally and technically adequate to the performance of adult roles."[110]

Child

Irvin L. Child (1954) defined "socialization" as "the whole *process by which an individual*, born with behavioral potentialities of enormously wide range, *is led* to develop actual behavior which is confined within a much narrower range—the range of what is customary and acceptable for him according to the standards of his group."[111]

This definition is unclear, above all because combined with "process" the term "led" is ambiguous. Usually "led" designates an action, but this sense is hardly compatible with the word "process," as some processes are not actions. Are educational actions meant here? Then only successful actions would fall under this concept, i.e., ones which have actually "led" (brought, caused) educands "to develop actual behavior" falling in the range of what is acceptable. We would in this case be dealing with a success concept of education.[112] Certain facts speak out against this interpretation, among others, that individuals can develop "actual behavior" (more precisely: acquire or develop psychic dispositions), even "behavior which is confined within . . . the range of what is customary and acceptable," without being "led" to do so, i.e., without being exposed to educational actions. Above all, the employment of a success concept of education presupposes that aims or purposes are present and that educational actions are performed for their sake. The "development of actual behavior" falling within the range of the acceptable is not an aim, because it is too imprecisely defined. A great variety of "actual behavior" (i.e., behavior without further specification) can develop without a person's being "led" by educational action to do so.

From the context it is apparent that Child in fact understands "socialization" as a synonym for "child rearing," "training" and education.[113] He suggests that "socialization is a matter of leading the child to learn something" and points to means including "techniques of punishment" and of reward.[114] Somewhat more vaguely he refers to "socialization" as "pressures exerted upon the child."[115] However, there is no doubt that Child means an *external influence*, "socialization as an influence on human behavior."[116]

Another reason for favoring this interpretation is that according to Child the concept of socialization "is closest to the concept of *education*." Socialization processes are "related to educational processes." "In theory" one can "*subsume* education as a term for specific special forms of the socialization process under *the higher concept of socialization*." However, already in the next sentence the relationship is reversed: "Education" is used as the higher-level concept, "socialization" as an "aspect of education." "In actual empirical practice" the concept of socialization has, according to Child, "assumed a somewhat more specialized meaning": it is used in referring to "those general human *aspects of education* which appear in life already before the beginning of formal education and . . . even during the period of formal education continue to occur in the family, in other communities and in the school."[117] Despite this contradiction we can at least recognize that he means roughly *influence* exerted by people on other persons: *influence, i.e., actions, which proceed from the intention of influencing other persons.* Beyond this everything remains vague.

Zigler and Child

Edward Zigler and Irvin L. Child (1969) offer the following definition: "Socialization is . . . the whole *process by which an individual develops*, through transaction with other people, his specific patterns of socially relevant behavior and experience."[118] This definition, offered as an improvement of Child's 1954 definition, names the "individual" as subject or bearer of the socialization process. Accordingly a different "process" seems to be intended than in the earlier definition, for a "process by which an individual . . . is *led* to develop . . . behavior" is quite obviously not the same as a "process by which an individual *develops* . . . his . . . behavior." In the first case it is a matter of an influencing process, in the second of a developmental process. The subject of an influencing process is a source of influence external to the individual; the subject of a developmental process is the developing individual. But the authors distance themselves from such simple empirical and logical considerations. Nowhere do they employ the socialization concept which they have defined, but rather they use "socialization" as a term for influences on children, especially "child-rearing practices" and their effects.

But given that Child's (or Zigler and Child's) definitions are often cited, we cannot simply dismiss the fact that the authors themselves do not hold to them, but rather we must at least examine their two most important conceptual attributes: the "process" and its results.

Let us assume that the attribute "process" refers to the process of *development*. Then "socialization" means the "whole process" through which a person acquires psychic dispositions for "socially relevant behavior and experience." This "*whole* process" (in the singular) is an invention, a hypothetical construction. In reality it does not exist. We can only find a sense for the concept "whole process" if it is understood as "the *sum* of all processes." Psychic dispositions for socially relevant behavior and experience certainly do not arise through only *one* process, but through the overall interaction within the person of many, to be sure quite hypothetical, processes. The occurrence of such processes is inferred when people are observed to perform "socially relevant behavior" which was not previously noted. The "socially relevant behavior and experience" (or the propensities or psychic dispositions underlying them) are viewed as "effects" which must have a "cause." This *supposed* (hypothetical) but *unknown* cause is called "socialization."

Zigler and Child's socialization concept thus has merely the following content: *the sum of the hypothetical processes in people through which they acquire psychic dispositions for socially relevant behavior and experience.* It should be clear that this concept, employed in reference to a posited sum total of unknown hypothetical processes, cannot at the same time also refer to the external conditions for these intra-subjective processes. "Socialization" in this sense is nothing more than a theoretical construct introduced to designate the sum of these processes. Closely related to the concept of the "becoming of personality," it is not an observable phenomenon. Nor is it an action: for to be an action it would require an aim or purpose.

The second conceptual attribute of Zigler and Child's socialization concept which deserves critical examination is the *result* of the sum of processes referred to as "socialization": "specific patterns of socially relevant behavior and experience." I will, however, not deal with the extremely vague term "pattern." The phrase does at least have a meaning if interpreted as referring to a class of behavioral and experiental *readinesses* (psychic dispositions). But which dispositions are intended?

This question can only be answered if we know what the authors understand "socially relevant" to mean. Our analysis of the ambiguous word "social" has shown that it can (among other things) mean "concerning society," "concerning groups of people," "concerning the relationships between or among (two or more) persons." Since we cannot exclude any of these senses as "not intended," the question arises: which parts of a person's behavioral repertoire are *irrelevant* to other people? Scarcely any could be named. At any rate, among those which are "socially relevant" we find not only community-furthering behaviors but also ones detrimental to the community, not only publicly useful behavior but also egoistic, aggressive and criminal behavior. This means, however, that most imaginable personality qualities (psychic dispositions) can be classified as "socially relevant." Thus we must assume that the result of socialization will be the following: *a person's psychic dispositional network* (or "personality"), *insofar as it is relevant for other people.*

Elkin

Frederick Elkin defines "socialization" as "the *process by which we learn* the ways of a given society or social group so that we can function within it."[119] In this definition the intended process is specified as a *learning* process. Elkin's conceptual attribute "to learn" is less vague than the attribute "to develop" used in Zigler and Child's definition. But the term "development" also appears in Elkin's discussion, as he further asserts that "socialization focuses" on those "aspects of development that concern the learning of and adaptation to the culture and society."[120] "Development" is just as ambiguous as "to develop."[121] In psychological studies it is usually defined to include "maturation processes," i.e., processes of the "ripening of innate behavioral tendencies in the absence of training and experience."[122] In psychology, "maturation" is the opposite of "learning," which is a psychic process leading through experience to the new acquisition or change of psychic dispositions for specific experiences or behaviors.[123]

Elkin's attempt in the above quote to interpret development in terms of "learning" is less enlightening than it might seem, since, like "development," learning processes are themselves hypothetical constructions. Not observable phenomena, they are assumed when we have determined that specific changes in the network of a person's experiential or behavioral propensities are not attributable to maturation processes.

For Elkin's conceptual attribute "process" (as a learning process) the same applies as for the attribute "process" (as a developmental process) in Zigler and Child's definition: there is no "*single* process" through which people learn the "ways" of their society, for the learning results they refer to come about only if *many* hypothetical but unknown learning processes occur. Thus here as well Elkin can only be reasonably understood to mean the *sum* of the hypothetical learning processes through which people acquire the psychic dispositions which enable them to be active members of their society.

Brim

Orville G. Brim defines "socialization" as "the *process by which persons acquire* the knowledge, skills, and *dispositions* that make them more or less able members of their society"[124] (I). Socialization is understood here as "acquisition" in the sense of "learning": "The individual acquires the culture of his group(s) through socialization"; he "learns, of course, role prescriptions and role behavior"; he acquires "habits, beliefs, attitudes, and motives," etc.[125] Brim states clearly that the results of this process are psychic dispositions ("knowledge" and "abilities," which he names as additional to "dispositions," are in fact also psychic dispositions). Brim does not, however, hold to his first conceptual definition, but employs the term "socialization" in two further senses.

Brim II: "Socialization" is a "*process by which society creates persons* suitable to carry out its functional requirements."[126] The statement: "society socializes the individual" is clarified with the assertion that society "transforms the raw material of biological man" or "changes the natural man."[127]

One cannot immediately tell from the action verbs "create," "transform" and "change" whether actions are intended which arise from the intention to create, transform and change. Since, however, "society" is named as the bearer of the process, thus an abstraction which in itself is unable to act, it can be assumed that here "socialization" is understood *as the sum of all processes* of *exerting influence originating in society* which contribute to bringing about "created," "transformed" or "changed" persons. This concept stands for the sum total of societal influencing processes which have brought about or helped to bring about the intended constitutions of the persons subjected to them. It could also include pur-

poseful influencing attempts (such as educational actions), but only if they have actually had an influence.

Brim III: Although this socialization concept is not expressly defined, it can, however, easily be reconstructed
from the author's usage. Brim writes that the individual
"receives" socialization.[128] He speaks of the "objective"
and of the "purposes" of socialization, of "socialization
methods," "socialization processes" and "socialization
technology."[129] Persons whom he calls "socializing a-
gents"[130] "socialize" people. An "agent" is a "person who
acts or exerts influence" (from the Latin "agentem," the
present participle of "agere," meaning to act). One can
only reasonably speak of "socializing agents" if "socialization" is understood as "action" and if "to socialize" is "to
act." Accordingly, the activities of these "agents" are primarily described with the words "to teach," "to instruct"
and "to train."[131]

We are thus dealing here under the name "socialization" with a *naive concept of education.* I call it naive because it is quite unrealistically assumed that the psychic
dispositions which "society creates" in the persons being
socialized are brought about through educational actions. To be sure, Brim occasionally mentions that "socializing agents" educate the objects of their "socialization efforts" not only consciously, intentionally and with
aforethought but also unintentionally and without planning.[132] Nowhere, however, is a clear distinction made
between education as a *conscious and purposeful attempt*
to exert influence and unintentional influences emanating from other people and from culture.

Clausen

John A. Clausen first states that he means by "socialization" a "kind of learning" which he calls "social learning."[133] He is, however, reluctant to define the term and
claims that the meaning of "socialization" can also be
represented by the following words: "child rearing, social
orientation of the child, education, enculturation, role
learning, occupational preparation, preparation for mar-

riage and parenthood, adaptation . . . socialization comprises all of these. . . . The concept of socialization embraces equally the *efforts* of society's formally designated socialization agents (parents, teachers, elders, preachers) *to transmit and secure adherence to existing norms* and the mutual efforts of participants in all sorts of relationships (peer group, courtship, marriage, work group) to establish stable expectations."[134]

Thus we have in this case a concept of socialization *combining* the two main classes of processes with which we have already become acquainted under the name "socialization": "social learning" *and* "the attempts of others to influence the individual."[135] Since Clausen takes into account that intentional attempts to influence can be unsuccessful or at least less effective than the "unintended consequences of the behavior of others," he thereby includes in socialization "*unwitting influences*" which stem from the behavior of other people. Added to this are actions which he terms "*self-socialization*," usually designated as "self-development" (or more problematically, "self-education"[136]).

For Clausen, "socialization" is thus a *higher-level concept for* the following four concepts: I. *social learning*, II. *education*, III. *unintentional processes of exerting social influence* and IV. *self-education*. It is surely possible to construct such a higher-level concept, but this would only give rise to misconceptions and errors. Confusion arises above all because the term "socialization" is employed not only in reference to the higher-level concept, but also to each of the lower-level concepts, i.e., to the classes of phenomena referred to by them. Social learning is termed "socialization," just as are education and unintentional processes of exerting social influence. Only the process of self-education is clearly distinguishable because of the modifier "self" in the expression "self-socialization."

The confusion is further multiplied if the verb "to socialize" is employed. It cannot be used at all to designate a process corresponding to the content of the higher-level concept, because such a vast process is inconceivable. If

"socialization" is intended to mean the lower-level concept "social learning," then the learner "socializes himself." If "education" is intended, then the educator "socializes" the person whom he wishes to induce to "socialize himself," i.e., cause to "learn socially." With this
sense, it can naturally also happen that the socializee
does *not* "socialize" himself (i.e., *does not* "learn socially"),
although his educator "socializes" him. If an "unintentional process of influencing" is meant, then—without
anyone intending this—it "socializes" a person who—influenced by the process—"socializes himself," i.e., "learns
socially."

Indeed the possibilities for confusion are still not ex-
hausted. Clausen namely also emphasizes that "every
enduring relationship may be said to entail socialization."[137] Again he says that socialization "entails a continuing interaction between the individual and those who
seek to influence him."[138] Now it is only possible to have
a "continuing interaction" when one is involved in an "enduring relationship." Clausen thus implies that the phenomenon which has "socialization" as a consequence also has "socialization" as a precondition. Put simply: "socialization" is everywhere, and everyone who participates
in an "enduring relationship" unavoidably "socializes"
and "is socialized."

We are confronted here with the revival of a conceptual confusion caused by a failure to differentiate concepts which burdened pedagogics more than sixty years
ago, when Ernst Krieck (a conservative German pedagogue, 1882-1947) claimed that "every formative interaction from person to person, every type . . . of action
which brings forth or influences becoming, structuring
and forming from wherever it originates" fell under his
concept of education. While at that time one could with
Krieck say: "Everyone is constantly educating everyone
else,"[139] today one can, if one follows the example of
Clausen, increase the confusion still more and say: "Everyone is constantly socializing everyone else and himself
as well."

Goslin

David E. Goslin, editor of an important handbook on this topic, offers no definition of "socialization," but only fragments from which readers must themselves reconstruct his understanding of the term. "Socialization," he asserts, involves "*preparation for participation in group life.*"[140] He uses the term above all when he means "*social learning.*" Anyone who studies "socialization" wants to discover "how individuals *learn to participate effectively in social interaction.*" Besides "social learning," he names "*child rearing*" and "*social development*" as socialization phenomena.[141]

The conceptual connections between these phenomena are established through the following line of reasoning. All new-born persons must acquire psychic dispositions enabling them to participate in group life. The acquisition of these dispositions "may occur as a result of *conscious efforts* on the part *of the society to teach* new members *or* as a result of *efforts* (both conscious and unconscious) on the part *of individuals to emulate* the behavior of others."[142] Accordingly Goslin's socialization concept includes not only the "means by which the external system exerts control over individual behavior," but also "the process of internalization, through which societal prescriptions and proscriptions become more or less autonomous energizers of behavior."[143]

In contrast to Clausen, whose socialization concept is to be understood as a higher-level concept for four lower-level concepts, Goslin thus means by "socialization" the *higher-level concept for* two concepts, "*education*" and "*social learning.*" Goslin is confusing in that he employs the word "socialization" for not only the higher-level concept, but also—without any explanatory comment—for each of the two lower-level concepts. Especially confusing is that he refers to "socialization *as a two-way process.*"[144] He intends thereby to say that not only does the "socializer" influence the "socializee," but the latter also influences the "socializer." This makes sense at best if "socialization" means education, for said of the process of social learning, which involves only a single person, it would mean that not only does the learner influence the learner, but the learner also influences the learner.

But even if "socialization" means education, "the conscious effort to teach," or the "means to control the behavior of other persons," speaking of "socialization as a two-way process" is inconsistent with other statements Goslin makes, because "socialization" was previously so defined that only a "one-way process" could fall under the concept: the process through which "society" (or the "external system," represented by the educator) *purposefully* and *consciously* teaches or exerts control over the behavior of an educand. By definition this logically rules out the possibility that any influencing processes initiated by educands and affecting their educators would fall under the concept of socialization. Given this presupposition it is thus also impossible that an object of socialization could simultaneously and within the same social relationship "socialize" his "socializer." Likewise precluded is the possibility that a "socializer" could simultaneously and within the same social relationship be an object of socialization. Of course not thereby disputed is that every social relationship is mutual and that accordingly not only does the educator actually influence the educand, but also the educand influences the educator and possibly even attempts consciously and purposefully to influence him.

Such contradictions inevitably arise if we forget that the *result* of socialization (*actual* in the case of social learning or *intended* in the case of education) belongs to the conceptual attributes of *all* socialization concepts: the psychic dispositions which make possible "participation in group life," etc. It is presupposed that "socializers" already possess these psychic dispositions. In contrast, the objects of socialization are assumed to be lacking and in need of acquiring them. "Socialization" understood as education means the actions through which educators attempt to stimulate, further or support necessary processes of "social learning" in their educands.

We could, by deviating from Goslin's own conceptual

explanation and from all the previously examined socialization concepts, intend "socialization" to mean nothing more than "influence exerted on a person by other persons" (without the influencer having an intention, aim or purpose to further those dispositions in influenced persons that make possible their "participation in group life"). Then we could say that, simultaneous with the socialization (i.e., here: education) to which they are exposed, the objects of socialization also "socialize" their "socializers." Even in this case it is, however, *not* a matter of *one and the same* process ("two-way process"), but rather of two "one-way processes" which can to some extent be co-determined by one another.

Inkeles

Alex Inkeles assumes that every individual is in a sense the result or product of a socialization process.[145] This product—regardless of how it is evaluated according to the currently valid norms of the particular society—depends on a series of production factors ("inputs"). To these belong the individual's hereditary constitution and all environmental factors including the personality constitutions of social partners, the culture of the relevant social environment, valid norms, education, etc. The term "socialization" designates at the same time three phenomena: *i.* "a *process*, or input, *external to the person*," *ii.* "*the individual's experience of the process*" and *iii.* "the *end product* or output." Expressed differently: "socialization" is here the name for a complex which consists of the personality, the process of its emergence (or becoming) and all the necessary internal and external conditions for this.

Inkeles distinguishes this, his broadest sense of the word (I), from a narrower one which is limited to the second of the three named classes of phenomena. "Socialization" in this sense "refers to *the sum total of past experiences* an individual has had which, in turn, may be expected to play some role in shaping his future social behavior."[146] This conceptual definition is reasonable if one starts from the product and wishes to refer to the processes that have occurred in the personality and thereby co-determined its production. Here we have a hypothetical construct, one applicable neither to the "experience" an individual is *currently* having (since by definition it is limited to *past* experiences) nor even to *real* "experiences," i.e., learning processes, which are indeed always limited, particular, individual and concrete. Yet combined these learning processes form the "sum total" of all experiences which alone make up the content of the concept.

In view of these inadequacies, it is scarcely surprising that Inkeles does not hold to his concept of socialization II, but tends more to view "socialization . . . as *socially relevant learning*" (III).[147] In general, he clearly demarcates this from the external "influences on the socialization process," comprising "a complex of forces" which "operates to produce the total socialization experience of each individual,"[148] forces including education, instruction, reward, punishment, etc. However, he also employs still a fourth concept of socialization: "Socialization is a relatively *conscious process of training* in anticipation of future social roles" (IV).[149] "The main business of socialization is the training of infants, children, adolescents (and sometimes adults) so that they can ultimately fulfill the social obligations that their society and culture will place on them."[150]

Secord and Backman

Paul F. Secord and Carl W. Backman provide the following definition: "Socialization is *an interactional process whereby* an individual's *behavior is modified* to conform to expectations held by members of the group to which he belongs" (I).[151] By "process" is meant here a "process of change" which occurs in the individual: the *process of* "*social learning*." This is understood as a learning process which brings about "changes in behavior and attitude having their origins in *interaction with other persons.*"[152]

"Communication through the mass media" is expressly included in the concept of "interaction," although—the authors mention as an example reading a book—in this case only an *action* on the part of the learner, but no *inter*action is possible. This expansion of the concept, incompatible as it is with the meaning of the word "interaction," suggests that the authors themselves apparently regard as questionable the limitation of "social learning" to the learning of dispositions "having their origins in interaction with other persons." If, however, in contradiction to the conceptual attribute "interaction with other persons" which they have themselves proposed, they wish to draw in learning processes co-determined by cultural phenomena such as the mass media, there is no reason to think that other non-"interactional" learning processes co-determined by cultural phenomena besides the mass media should not be taken into account. To more precisely specify the learning process as "interactional" is questionable anyway, because it can hardly be proved that specific attitudinal and behavioral changes have "their origins in interaction with other persons."[153]

Even more confusing is the following inconsistency. Secord and Backman define the ambiguous expression "social learning" as a learning process which brings forth learning results "having their origins in interaction with other persons." In other words: "social learning" is present if learning results can be attributed to the interaction of the learner with other persons. In this conceptual definition of "social learning" no account is taken of the sorts of learning results produced and how they are evaluated by the learner's group. The propensities to hatred, lying, laziness, more generally: to deviant behavior, fall under this concept just as much as do propensities for behavior consistent with norms, insofar as it can be assumed that such behaviors have their "origins in interaction with other persons." Now for Secord and Backman, "socialization" is "social learning." But according to their definition, "socialization" can only mean a learning process giving rise to behavior in conformity "with expectations held by members of the groups" to which a learner belongs. Thus in this case there is a limitation to learning which produces results positively evaluated by these groups.

This inconsistency arises because, in addition to the concept of "social learning" explicated by the authors (as learning in "social" situations or in interaction with social partners), they employ still another concept without explicitly introducing and explaining it: "Social learning" means in this case the learning of behavioral propensities which "conform with expectations held by members of the groups" to which learners belong, i.e., psychic dispositions for behavior in accord with norms.

It would only be possible to avoid this problem if the authors defined "socialization" not as identical with "social learning I" (learning in interaction), but as a subconcept of "social learning I." This would designate that subset of processes of "social learning I" leading to behavioral propensities that "conform with the expectations held by members of the groups" to which learners belong ("social learning II," the learning of propensities for "social" behavior). In this case "social" behavior means behavior in accord with group norms. "Socialization" could then be understood as a process of learning in interaction with other persons through which behavioral readinesses are acquired that enable learners to comply with the expectations (norms) of the groups to which they belong.

It must be pointed out that Secord and Backman also offer a second definition of socialization differing from the one previously explained: "the processes by which . . . the relation of the individual to other persons . . . develop are known as socialization" (II).[154] This hardly suggests anything in particular, but at any rate an entirely different hypothetical object seems to be meant here than a learning process through which psychic dispositions are developed for behavior in accord with norms.

Finally, "socialization" is defined a third time as a "*process of change occurring throughout the life career* of an individual as a result of his *interactions with other persons*" (III).[155] In this definition there is a no reference to any results or to provisional results of this process of change in the personalities of those who experience it. The process can only be characterized as "social" (as an allusion to the word "socialization"), because it is conditioned by "interaction with others" (more realistically one would probably have to say: *co*-conditioned). It would be hard to imagine a concept of socialization which would be poorer in content.

EXAMPLES FROM GERMAN SOCIALIZATION LITERATURE

Wurzbacher

Gerhard Wurzbacher understands "socialization . . . as a *process of guiding, caring for and imprinting the person by* the behavioral expectations and behavioral control of his *relational partners.*"[156] Elsewhere he omits the attributes "guiding" and "caring for" and characterizes "socialization" as "*social imprinting*"[157] or as a "process of societalizing imprinting of a person by the group."[158] In addition to "imprinting," he also speaks of "a life-long *forming*" and "moulding."[159] Further he states that "socialization" is the "integration of the person into the social group."[160] "Society" is named as the "bearer of socialization": "it forces him to integrate and subordinate . . . himself . . . and . . . to become . . . a role bearer." It confronts people "through its various social patterns . . . and role bearers . . . demanding, rewarding and punishing with inescapable pressure to adapt."[161] Rather than small groups, he designates large groups, the "national and international large associations," and "secondary systems" as the "dominant bearers of socialization."[162]

This concept of socialization is unclear, because its contents are designated with undefined and in general usage vague terms like "guiding," "caring for," "imprinting," "forming," "moulding" and "integrating." The words "guiding" and "caring for" are usually employed in reference to purposeful action. "Guiding" means showing the way, directing someone's actions;[163] "to care for" means

to look after, provide for or supervise a person.[164] The
reference to the "behavioral control of his relational partners" could be interpreted in such a way that in this case
"socialization" is intended to mean education. As well,
"imprinting" could be understood as purposeful action,
for "to imprint" means "to produce or impress (a mark or
pattern) on a surface," "to produce a vivid, often favorable effect on the mind or emotions," "to establish firmly
in the mind."[165] However, "imprinting," just as well as
"forming" or "moulding," can mean an unintentional process of influencing. Among the reasons for not interpreting it as purposeful action are that "socialization" is referred to as a "lifelong" process, and "lifelong" actions do
not happen in the real world; further, that "secondary
systems" are named as the "dominant bearers of socialization," and they, at any rate, can perform no educational or other actions on individual persons; and finally,
that actions can also be unsuccessful, while in this case
the *effects* of socialization processes are definitionally
presupposed, so that at least unsuccessful actions are
excluded. Wurzbacher thus seems to mean by "socialization" the sum of influencing processes which arise from a
person's social environment. Perhaps he also includes
educational actions, although he does not mention them,
but merely speaks vaguely of "guiding" and "caring for."
The only thing certain is that a process of influencing
persons from outside is intended, or more precisely, the
sum of such processes.

Claessens

Dieter Claessens understands by "socialization" the "*process of transmitting and receiving socio-cultural contents.*"
He clarifies this as a process "in which *influences are exerted* on individuals and *received* by them in such a way
that that they 'master' the behavioral structures or patterns inherent in these influences."[166] He also calls this a
"comprehensive process of value transmission between
society and individual"[167] or a "process of handing down
culture."[168] Thus this concept of socialization (I), similar

to Inkeles I, comprehends phenomena ranging from processes of influencing the individual to the latter's learning processes to the appearance of signs that the transmitted contents have been successfully assimilated into his behavioral repertoire.

We find, however, that Claessens also employs three further socialization concepts. "Socialization" is namely also subsumed under the higher-level concept of *learning* and defined by him as "*internalization*," i.e., as the acquisition through learning of the "behavior of parents or educators" (II).[169] Further, he employs "socialization" in the sense of "forming and educating processes" (III),[170] and also calls the "process of socialization" simply "education."[171] Finally, according to Claessens even "the (new) *internalized behavioral modes* can be designated with the concept of 'socialization'" (IV).[172]

Neidhardt

Friedhelm Neidhardt defines "socialization" as the "*transmission or transfer of behavioral dispositions* by socializers" to socializands (I). "In this process" there are "on the side of the socializand: learning . . . on the side of the socializer: demonstration as well as pressure through reward or punishment."[173]

If we take this definition literally, we find a concept being defined which in no way corresponds to reality. A "transmission or transfer of behavioral dispositions" from one person to another is impossible—unless one means that through the act of procreation parents transmit to their offspring the genetic *potential* for behavior. Behavioral dispositions cannot be transmitted. If a person *a* wants another person *b* to acquire specific behavioral dispositions similar to ones which person *a* has already acquired, he can only *attempt* through personal actions to influence the conditions for them to arise in *b*. Such influence attempts can, however, also have quite different effects from those desired, or they can be unsuccessful. Use of the words "transmit" or "transfer" suggests a non-existent nomological cause-and-effect relationship between the behavior of the "socializer" and the appearance of the dispositions he wants to establish in the object of socialization. This hypothetical relationship is then alleged to account for changes in the dispositions and accordingly for the behavior of the object of the "transmission" or "transfer" efforts (or "socialization efforts"[174]).

The word "transmit" means "to send from one person, thing, or place to another"; "convey; "to cause to spread; pass on"; to "impart or convey to others by heredity"; to "send" a signal. "Transfer" means "to convey or shift from one person or place to another"; "to convey . . . from one surface to another."[175] If one remains consistent with these senses, then Neidhardt could really only mean "socialization" in the sense of an action (or a series of actions) employed by an transmitter as a means to bring about a desired effect in the object of the action. As well the name "socializer" for the acting subject indicates that "socialization" is understood as an action whose originator or bearer is a person as an acting subject. Since in clarifying his definition Neidhardt speaks of a "process" which includes "learning" on the part of the object of action, it must be assumed, however, that like Inkeles I and Claessens I, he intends the whole range of processes extending from the action of the acting subject to the appearance of desired behavior in the object of the action. Besides this sense, however, we come across two further ones.

Neidhardt II: "The concept of socialization designates *the learning of* the dominant *behavioral norms* of society and its respective subgroups." "It includes *all* learning processes, not only those which derive from intentional educational influences."[176] Here "socialization" is defined as a learning process. Instead of "behavioral dispositions," as in the first definition, he names "behavioral norms." Since norms in themselves are of a different nature than psychic dispositions, in this case Neidhardt presumably means learning processes leading to knowledge of norms and the propensity to obey or to behave in accord with them.

Neidhardt III: "socialization means *social influence* on the personalities of socializands."[177] Because the ambiguous conceptual attribute "influence" is employed, what is intended is not any clearer: (a) an effect which people *unintentionally* have on other people, (b) an action by means of which a person *purposefully attempts* to influence other people, whereby it remains open whether the intended effect appears, (c) an influence attempt to the extent that it produces *any sort* of effect, (d) a concept subsuming not only effects in sense *a*, but also influence attempts in sense *c*, (e) or an influence attempt if and only if it *produces* the *intended* effect?

From the context one learns that Neidhardt usually means sense IIIe: "the *process through which the values, norms and life techniques* valid in the social environment *are transmitted to and made binding on* the individual."[178] He speaks of "socialization aims," of the "socialization program," of "socialization success," of the "technique of socialization" and of "socialization practices" which "socializers employ."[179] These expressions make sense only if by "socialization" is meant educational actions in which the "socializer" is understood to be an educator and the "socializand" to be an educand.

This concept of socialization is perplexing, in that it presupposes and encourages the illusion that "socialization" (understood as education) is always successful, so that *actions* through which the *attempt* is made to transmit values, norms and life techniques can be understood as making up a "process" "through which" these values, norms and techniques are *actually* also "transmitted and made binding." The entire conceptual confusion is rooted in the naive confusion of that which the "socializer" does and can "create" with the "genesis" of psychic dispositions in the educand which the "socializer" values and wants to "bring about," although he cannot in fact "create" them, but can at best, as one among many conditions, only indirectly contribute to creating them.

Habermas

To explain his socialization concept, Jürgen Habermas takes a position which brings him close to Parsons's use of role theory: "In the course of the *learning process* called socialization, potentially action-capable subjects internalize the value orientations and develop the motivations which enable them to play social roles."[180] In contrast to Parsons and many other authors, he holds consistently to this concept and does not give cause to terminologically confuse socialization as a learning process with the societal conditions for this process. He consistently names as the subject of socialization the person who "*acquires*" the "action ability" or "basic qualifications," "*learns*" roles, "*adopts* and . . . internalizes the normative expectations of another subject."[181] Accordingly the "educational techniques" or the "educational behavior" of parents (and other educators) are throughout unambiguously represented as social conditions for socialization processes (or for the "genesis of motivations" or for "cognitive and linguistic development").[182]

Mollenhauer

Klaus Mollenhauer writes that "the term socialization comprehends all *learning processes* whose results constitute a human organism as a member of a society." Stated in greater detail it refers to "the learning processes . . . through which a human organism acquires those behavioral qualifications necessary in order to be able to communicate in groups, institutions and as occupants of social positions with other members of society" (I). The acquired "qualifications" are a matter above all "of the common value orientations of the culture and society and their internalization, of the motives for action."[183]

Here "socialization" is unambiguously defined as a sum of learning processes and thereby as a sum of *psychic processes*. In general, Mollenhauer clearly distinguishes between socialization and its conditions.[184] Among the "socialization conditions" are also "educational practices."[185] Mollenhauer rightly points out that the socialization process must not be conceived as a self-contained process "whose form and manner could only be described with the aid of endogenous variables. As a *social process* it must also, not only as a whole, but also in its individual moments, be viewed as a dependent variable in the total constellation of societal influences."[186] The socialization process is dependent on the character of "socialization agents" and on socio-economic factors, etc. Mollenhauer thus means by "socialization" a *psychic process* co-determined by social factors. That in this case he also designates it as a "*social* process" (instead of more precisely: as a societally *conditioned* psychic process) seems attributable to mere carelessness in his choice of terms.

Despite his efforts to distinguish in a terminologically clear manner between the process of socialization and its conditions, Mollenhauer frequently also employs the word "socialization" in the sense of "*education*" (II). He speaks of "socialization practices" when he means "educational practices," of "socialization praxis" in the sense of "educational praxis," of "modes of socialization" and "socialization style" when he means education as a *condition* of socialization.[187]

Fend

Helmut Fend, with regard to social science usage, distinguishes between "socializing as making social" and "socializing as becoming social." The first concept refers to "the sum of all activities of influencing persons," the second, to "the transformation and construction of the personality on the basis of socio-cultural influencing." "In the first case, a person offers cultural contents, in the second case, a person learns cultural contents."[188] Since the term "education" is already used in the first sense, but, to the contrary, a term has previously been lacking for the second sense, Fend suggests, following Brezinka, that the term "socialization" be employed exclusively for "*becoming social*" as a "*subprocess in the becoming of the personality.*"[189] He emphasizes that this concept has "the logical character of a complicated theoretical construct" whose sense is only realized within a theoretical frame of reference encompassing the interrelationship between social influencing and the personality's becoming. Not describing "socialization" in terms of observable phenomena, he points to "unobservable, but inferable relationships between the objects of observations."[190]

Accordingly "socialization" (socializing) means for Fend "*the learning of valuations and norms*" (I).[191] He offers this definition: "Socialization means the process by which an individual is integrated into a society or one of its groups through a process of learning the norms and values of the respective group and society."[192] The word "integration" is ambiguous and can be used transitively for the act through which individuals are integrated by others or intransitively for the process through which individuals integrate themselves into society. Since Fend understands "*socialization . . . as a learning process*," it seems clear that for him "integration into society" means the process of integrating oneself. "In the process of socialization . . . norms and value systems (sexual mores, codes of correct behavior, political value systems, Weltanschauung) are learned and internalized."[193]

Fend did not, however, stick to his socialization concept I, but formulated another which includes not only intra-personal learning processes, but also influencing processes through which "socialization agents" produce learning processes. The truism that "the process of socialization simultaneously fulfills important functions for the individual and society" (which he calls "the thesis of the double function of the socialization process"),[194] caused him to not only broaden his field of view to "the problem of the reproduction of society," but also to expand his original concept of socialization. While in Fend I the individual is the subject of his socialization (as a learning process), in Fend II society occupies the center of the stage as the subject of an influencing process. Fend explains that "in every case the socialization process is a matter of *enabling individuals* through learning processes . . . to become bearers of social systems."[195] The learning process which formed the central conceptual attribute in Fend I is in Fend II a mere part of the socialization process, one without which societally desired dispositions cannot be acquired. In the foreground is now the "*process of social influencing*," and learning processes are "complementary" to them, because the "state of consciousness, need systems and action patterns" of new members of society cannot be "constructed" by society other than "through learning processes" or "through the process of learning."[196]

Besides this socialization concept II, in which influencing and learning are combined as "complementary" processes, Fend employs yet a third: "socialization" as education (III). Only if one means "*socialization as making social*" is it logically admissible to speak of "socialization *agencies*"[197] which offer "access to the social influencing of the younger generation," of the "socializer,"[198] of the "self-understanding of the participants in the socialization process"[199] or of the "social system into which [people] are socialized."[200] Only if one means "education" when one says "socialization" does it make sense to speak of "the *aims of the socialization process*, for example, in the form of parental educational aims or school educational aims"[201] and to ask: "which *aims* are formulated in schools *for socialization*, what, for example, are the conceptions of the ideal person . . . set down in curricula and guidelines?"[202] The same thing applies if the school system is referred to as the "domain of arranged socialization" or "educational institutions" as "planned institutions for the socialization and training of the younger generation."[203]

Thus for Fend the term "socialization" means at least three concepts. Since this fact does not seem obvious to the author himself, the reader is given no terminological aid in distinguishing among them. The fateful consequence for theory building of this conceptual confusion is that no clear distinction is made between education as an *attempt* at influencing, the actually effective social influencing processes and learning processes in educands.

If for example one speaks of the "concrete arrangement of socialization,"[204] then it makes a considerable difference whether one is thinking in this case of "Socialization III" (education) or "Socialization I" (learning). The "arrangement of education" is possible, while the "arrangement of learning" is not. This is because one cannot "arrange" psychic processes from without, but at most stimulate them. If the same word "socialization" is employed for both processes, then this ambiguous and inconsistent terminological usage, something to be frowned on in science, seduces us to mistakenly assume that the impossible could really be possible. Instead of investigating actual relationships, a distorted picture of reality is constructed and promulgated.

Such a distorted picture arises of necessity if education as an influence *attempt* is confused with an actually effective social influencing process, as continually happens in Fend's writings. That the learning processes called "socialization" by Fend "correspond"[205] to social influencing processes (i.e., are in accord with, related to or conditioned by them) or that both sorts of processes are "complementary"[206] is correct purely by definition: an actually effective social influencing process can only be referred to by an effect concept. The effectiveness of the process is inferred from an observable change in the person influenced, which is thought to result from a hypothetical learning process. With more or less justification the observed change is attributed to this learning process. Conversely: if "socialization" understood as "social learning," is so defined that by "social" is meant not (or not solely) the sorts of things learned (social or societally relevant dispositions), but rather learning "through interaction and communication processes"[207] with social partners, then it follows by definition that "socialization" presupposes "social influencing" and is always (co)determined by it. Such merely definitionally established truth must not, however, be confused with empirical knowledge of which social influencing processes co-determine which learning processes in what manner.

Above all, however, a "social influencing process" is

not the same as an influencing *attempt*. A distinction must be made between "socialization as *making* social" and the *attempt* to "make" another social (an intentional concept of education instead of an effect concept[208]). A specific real educational action *can*, if it has *demonstrably* brought about a change in an educand, be referred to *after its occurrence* as an actually effective "social influencing process" (which does not, however, by any means prove that it was successful, i.e., that it had the *specific* effect which was intended by the educator). As long as this proof is lacking, an educational action is to be viewed as no more than an influencing *attempt*. To speak of influencing *attempts* as though they were actually effective influencing processes is to merely definitionally credit these attempts with success in bringing about what one wants to achieve by their means. This amounts to deceiving oneself and others. It implies a power of disposal over psychic processes in educands which "socializers" and "agents of socialization" in reality do not possess.

Roth

Heinrich Roth first states, in *Pedagogical Anthropology* (Pädagogische Anthropologie, 1971), that "*learning processes*" are subsumed "under the collective concept of 'socialization'." He understands "the processes of socialization as *adaptive processes*"[209] or as "*learning processes*" (I).[210]

Just a few lines further on in the text he sees himself "forced to call . . . *the indirect societal regulators* of the functional educational field . . . socialization" (II).[211] By a "functional educational field" he understands "the field of relations among people" (but also among people and "things"), which is "always laden with mutual influencing tendencies." "The functional educational field is filled with all inhibiting and furthering forces and powers which consciously or unconsciously are at work among people and among people, things and tasks." In this "field" can be found "biological self-regulations" and "societal regulators." The latter are specified as "societal forces," ones "which regulate . . . the life and social field." "Education exists, because the two [biological and societal regulators] are insufficient."[212]

Thus in this explanation phenomena are called "socialization" which are not learning processes, but rather possible *external socio-cultural conditions* for specific psychic dispositions to arise as the result of learning processes. Furthermore, "regulators" can hardly refer to influencing *processes*, but we must probably suppose that what is meant is something like a *source* of influencing or an influencing *factor* from which influencing processes emanate. Roth does not explain the nature of "*indirect* societal regulators," and it is also hard to infer, because "direct" regulators are never mentioned. We can only be certain that "education" is not subsumed under this concept of socialization, and indeed for two reasons: first, "socialization" is defined here as a "regulator," while "education" is always understood as a process or action; second, education is referred to as something added to "socialization," if or because the latter "is insufficient."

On the same page Roth speaks of a "*complex . . . which we call social development, socialization and social education*" (III).[213] From the context one can hardly judge whether Roth employs the three expressions in the same sense and thus regards them as mutually substitutable, or whether he means a "complex" thought of as combining the sum of "social development," "socialization" and "social education" as three different elements. Here he states that he wants to determine the nature of the "components" of the "socialization process," "which can be regarded as particular dimensions of learning processes and which through reciprocal influence compose the complex which we call social development, socialization and social education." Given the wording, one is forced to assume that in this case Roth views the expressions "social development," "socialization" and "social education" as three names for one and the same thing. This would, however, be so anomalous that one is reluctant to take it seriously. On the other hand, however, it is clear that

Roth intends to work out the "components" of "learning processes," that is of "socialization processes," and that these "reciprocally interacting" elements "make up the complex" whose "components" he is endeavoring to explain. Thus in this case the "complex" referred to can only be a complex of "socialization processes" and not one thought to be composed of these processes along with the two further classes of phenomena, "social development" and "social education." In fact, then, we seem to be dealing not with "socialization" as a higher-level concept for the three concepts of "social development," "socialization" and "social education," but rather with "socialization" as a synonym for each of these three expressions, thereby presupposing their semantic equivalence (for Roth). "Socialization" in this case is not only "social development" (IIIa), but also "social education" (IIIb), although it is not, however, a higher-level concept under which both can be subsumed. A greater conceptual confusion is scarcely imaginable.

The word "socialization" is also used by Roth in a fourth sense: he refers thereby to *the result of learning and education in the person of the educand* (IV). "Learning through identification," "together with the . . . behavioral steering which emanates from parents," is what brings about "the socialization of the child."[214]

Finally, Roth also understands "socialization" as "*education*" (V). He writes of the "dependence of all learning processes on socializing and teaching processes"[215] and of "external controls through the socializing and educating process."[216] If "learning processes" are dependent on "socializing processes," then obviously "socialization" cannot be intended to mean socialization as a learning process (Roth I). Speaking of "external controls through the socialization process" makes sense only if one neither replaces the word "socialization" with "learning process" (Roth I) nor with "societal regulator" (which is certainly not a process: Roth II), but instead assumes that "education" is intended.

Kuckartz

Wilfried Kuckartz explicitly promises "a conceptual clarification" of the problem of "socialization and education."[217] Strangely, however, he does not start from the
fact that the word "socialization" is employed in several
senses, but writes about *the* concept of socialization as
though there were only one.[218] This single concept is his
own, which he defines as follows: "Socialization should
*be called the process of formation through societal behav-
ioral expectations and controls.*"[219]

Kuckartz presupposes that everyone knows the meaning of "formation"[220] and leaves this central conceptual
attribute completely unexplained. Little is said in lexica
about this word. We learn from them only that "to form"
(from the Latin "formare," to shape, form, develop, create,
bring forth, prepare[221]) means "to give form to"; "shape";
to "mold into a particular form"; "to fashion, train, or develop by instruction or precept"; "to constitute or compose an element, part, or characteristic of"; "to develop in
the mind; conceive."[222] "Formation" means "the process
of forming or producing." In the military a formation is a
"specified arrangement or deployment" of troops, while in
geology it refers to "a succession of strata."[223] From the
context we can, however, assume that Kuckartz means
something like "forming through social influences" or
"taking on a form" as a "process of forming." Just who
the object of this process could be, thus who takes on a
form or is "formed," remains, however, unstated, but
there can be scarcely any doubt that a person or individual is intended.

Kuckartz emphasizes that "intentional education" is
also an aspect of "socialization," and thus "the concept of
socialization . . . includes that of education."[224] Besides
intentional education it also includes so-called "functional education."[225] This can be understood as referring to
processes which form people (or to an influencing process), one which elicits effects in the persons influenced
coinciding with conceived personality states set as educational aims. Such a process is thought to occur with-

out any intention of bringing about the effects produced. Accordingly then, "socialization" means here a *combination of education and the unintended influencing process* (insofar as this process leads to results in the influenced person corresponding to societal "behavioral expectations"). Kuckartz states that "education" is the "conscious and planned part" of the "process of formation."[226] In place of the word "formation" he also uses the word "influence."[227] "Socialization" accordingly means in this case the "*social formation*" *of the person* or "*social influence*" *on people* (I), whereby the word can refer not only to intended, but also to unintended formation or influence.

Kuckartz explains this process at length as "formation," in the sense of "education" and external "influencing." However, at the end of his book he suddenly emphasizes that socialization is a *process of "learning"* (II). It is, as such, "different from formation through maturation, i.e., endogenous, species-specific developmental processes."[228] If we take this seriously, we are forced to substitute the word "learning" in every case where Kuckartz speaks of "socialization." This leads to statements of the following sort: "The concept of learning includes that of education"; "Education is the conscious and planned part of learning"; "Education is rationalized learning,"[229] etc. The absurdity of these statements shows that in "socialization as learning"—apparently without himself noticing it—Kuckartz has introduced a second concept of socialization, which is incompatible with his first one.

Even if one ignores this contradiction and holds to "Socialization I" as "social influencing," there still remains a great deal of conceptual confusion to clear up. The reason for this is that Kuckartz has *combined an effect concept with an intentional concept.*[230] The "effect concept" is in this case one which postulates that an unintended influencing process has produced or helped to produce a personality attribute corresponding to societal behavioral expectations. Effect concepts of this sort are misleadingly called "functional education." By "intentional concept" I mean here "intentional *education*" involving attempts at influencing. "Socialization" as an unintentional influencing process can only be identified by inferring back from a realized effect to the process which has conditioned it. "Socialization" in this sense is thus always effective and is always "functioning socialization."[231] "Socialization" as ("intentional") education, to the contrary, is purposeful action. It is an intentional *attempt* at influencing whose effect is unforeseeable and must therefore also be left out of account in the concept itself. In this sense "socialization" may or may not succeed. If "socialization" is employed, as in Kuckartz I, as a higher-level concept for (a) effective but unintended influencing processes and (b) intentional but possibly ineffective (more exactly: unsuccessful) actions, then confusion and error are scarcely to be avoided.

Take for example the statement, "education is . . . rationalized socialization,"[232] which Kuckartz proposes following Durkheim's questionable formulation of education as "methodical socialization" (French: socialisation méthodique).[233] One can scarcely refrain when reading or hearing such a statement from involuntarily (associatively) thinking of the subconcept "Socialization Ia." Thus education appears to be an action which always (regularly or usually) inevitably (or almost so) brings about whatever one wants it to produce, just as "socialization," as an unintended influencing process, is inevitably effective (simply by definition). Kuckartz does, to be sure, occasionally mention that intentional "socialization or education" does "not imply success eo ipso,"[234] but that is easily forgotten if one pursues the "methodization of functioning socialization"[235] and suggests "using socialization and education synonymously."[236] Misunderstandings will at any rate be more easily avoided by assigning different names to different concepts instead of lumping them together under a single name, an arbitrarily constructed amalgam of two incompatible ideas which almost no one will recognize for what it is. When such a composite term is created, some persons will see it as referring to one of its components, while some will suppose that it refers to the other.

Fröhlich

Werner Fröhlich assumes that there is neither a unified concept nor a unified theory of the phenomenon called "socialization." "Socialization is the title of a highly complex process which can be viewed under numerous aspects."[237] He refers to "*a behavior modifying (learning) process* resting on an orientation to an existing 'culture.' This orientation is accomplished—more precisely conceived—by taking into account expectations emanating from society."[238] "It is a matter of a process in whose course someone—regardless of age—learns to relate his behavior and experience to the behavior and experience of other people. The 'others' thereby remain relatively anonymous. Congealed forms, e.g., group norms . . . replace them and serve as guidelines for action."[239]

What is essential is that "socialization" cannot be observed in either people's experience or behavior, but is an "ideal type construct," an "ideal type setting," i.e., a "designation for an assumed process, thus a hypothetical process variable."[240] More exactly expressed, it is a matter of "the designation for a complex, abstractly formulated and general . . . *network of hypothetical process variables.*"[241] This process can only be demarcated from all other psychic processes by making reference to its results (to *what* is learned), not, however, by drawing on "how" (in "social interaction"). Fröhlich's concept of socialization is so defined that it can only be employed in cases where a predefined end state is achieved. Socialization can then be understood as that *subaspect in the* "*total process of* maturation and learning-conditioned changes of somatic and psychic characteristics" ("*development*") resting on interaction which, "seen in relationship to an *end state*, is characterized by the formation of individually and *socially relevant behavioral and experiental modes.*"[242]

The hypothetical process of socialization "can be more closely characterized as *implicit or explicit learning*" which "commences—one can assume—through at first asymmetrical and later gradually more symmetrical, reciprocal dependencies on and relationships with other people. It leads to the formation or construction of societally relevant behavioral and experiental schemata." By "asymmetrical" is meant that an interaction "is impossible because of an individual's level of development or maturation: societal relationships are symmetrical if the interaction partners can fully orient themselves in their (social) environment so that equilibrium or near equilibrium can be assumed as the starting position of the interaction."

The result of socialization is described by Fröhlich as "the more or less successful, objective and realistic evaluation of one's own relationship to the social environment" and the "possibility" arising from it "to call forth such, and above all such modes of behavior and experience which not only correspond to respective personal wishes and needs, but also take into account the—perhaps different and competing—wishes and needs of one or another fellow human beings."[243]

This concept of socialization definitely excludes processes other than those of learning. Anyone who uses it is terminologically protected from confusing learning processes with their postulated conditions. There is no place in theories employing this concept for "socializers," "socialization agencies," "socializands," "socialization aims" and acts of "socializers." Fröhlich's concept can also protect us from the illusion that there is a linear and monocausal dependency relationship between the results of socialization and those attempts at influencing which one usually calls "education."

Rössner

Lutz Rössner first roughly defines "socialization" as *socially specific (socially relevant) learning.*" Since he understands "learning" as the "acquisition or change of dispositions through the processing of information," "socialization" means for him: "acquisition or change of dispositions through the processing of socially specific (socially relevant) information." Here the attribute "socially specific" is related to the "input" of information. Accordingly the learning of all possible dispositions appears to fall under this concept. However, Rössner obviously means the "acquisition or change of *socially specific* (socially relevant) dispositions," i.e., the attribute "socially specific" must primarily be related to "output." One such output, "socially specific learning," is indeed later explained as learning "whose *effects* . . . are evaluated by societal authorities." "Since in principle *every* learning effect (and thus implicitly also every learning process) can be evaluated by societal authorities," it appears that "*all learning is potentially socialization.*"[244]

Accordingly one must assume that learning processes leading to results negatively evaluated by "societal authorities" also come under Rössner's concept of socialization. However, he precludes this possibility by introducing a further attribute. In his "ultimate" conceptual definition "socialization" is defined as "the acquisition or change of dispositions through the processing of socially specific information with the effect that the socializand realizes behavioral modes which are *evaluated* by a societal authority *as fulfilling its norms.*"

He distinguishes this from the concept of "*dissocialization,*" which he defines as the "acquisition or change of dispositions through the processing of socially specific information with the effect that the dissocializand realizes modes of behavior which are evaluated by a societal authority as deviating from its norms." As an explanation Rössner adds: "We are dealing in cases of socialization and in cases of dissocialization with the same learning processes; we only refer to the same process differently, on the mere basis of the *evaluations* which, with reference to the effects of these processes, are realized by societal authorities." Accordingly it is possible "that the same learning process is designated by one societal authority as socialization and by another societal authority as dissocialization."[245]

It is clear to Rössner that the concept of socialization is an "effect concept": "whether the individual . . . has undergone . . . socialization . . . can only be said on the basis of the determined and evaluated effect."[246] He leaves no doubt that education has a trial character. Nevertheless in attempting to explicate the relationship between socialization and education he becomes entangled in contradictions. Rössner explains "education" as an attempt "to influence socializations" or "to so steer a socialization that this socialization has an effect which can be positively evaluated by the educator."[247] Now, however, according to Rössner's definition, "socialization" means nothing other than a learning process leading to a learning result "judged by a societal authority" (educators are also included under this vague concept[248]) "as fulfilling its norms." Among the norms which come into consideration here are also educational aims.[249] If a learning result is judged as "fulfilling" an educational aim, this means that the aim has been achieved (or that the educand has at least come sufficiently close to realizing the educational aim). Thus accordingly, where "socialization" is present, education is superfluous. Since Rössner's concept of "socialization" already implies that it always has a positively evaluated result, no attempt at all by an educator is needed "to steer a socialization so that it has an effect which can be positively evaluated by the educator."

Given Rössner's conceptual presuppositions, even the concept which he himself formulated of "*educationally steered socialization*" makes no sense. It is defined as a "socially specific and socially relevant learning process which is so influenced by the conveying of information, planned by a person *s1*, that the effect of this learning process is positively evaluated by *s1*." Just as unusable is his definition of "education" as a "conveying of information planned by a person *s1* and directed at a person *s2* with the aim of influencing the socialization of *s2* so that *s2* retains, acquires or changes his dispositions [with the result] that *s2* realizes behavior fulfilling the behavioral expectations (norms) of *s1* (and/or his employer)."[250]

In both definitions the author assumes the possibility

that "socialization," if it is not "educationally steered" or "influenced," might possibly also *not* be "socialization," i.e., might *not* lead to learning results positively evaluated by a "societal authority." This is, however, *excluded on definitional grounds*, for Rössner's concept of "socialization" also includes as a conceptual attribute the stipulation that in every case (without exception) the underlying hypothetical learning process leads to positively evaluated learning results. The concept was formed on the basis of this positively evaluated learning result, i.e., "socialization" as a hypothetical process was invented to provide an intellectual aid. Its introduction appears justifiable because it enables us to explain the presence of positively evaluated psychic dispositions.

If we remember that "socialization" is not an observable process, not an empirical phenomenon, but rather a hypothetical object, an ideal type construct, we will avoid falling prey to the error that "socialization" can be "steered." The term "to steer" implicitly exaggerates educators' ability to influence and thus cannot serve as an explanation of what is actually possible for educators to do. It gives the false impression that the "steersman" or "pilot" (educator) has a much greater power of disposal over the "steeree" (educand) than is the case in actual practice.[251] Furthermore, even if we assumed that we could "steer" people, we cannot "steer" "socialization"—as defined by Rössner—because "socialization" is not at all steerable. It is nothing other than a hypothetical learning process whose result has been established by definition. Since whenever one uses this concept of "socialization" the learning result must be thought of as already present, there is no possibility at all of intervening from without in order to "steer" socialization toward the already present learning result, or even toward one deviating from this defined result.

This example demonstrates how easily confusion can arise when we try to bring "education" as a concept for real action into a relationship with "socialization" as a concept for a hypothetical learning process occurring in educands, one defined on the basis of specific learning results. While the character of the learning process termed "socialization" is invariant, simply due to the inclusion of learning results in the definition of socialization, from the educator's viewpoint what is of interest is precisely the educand's variability (indeterminacy or pliability), his opportunity, ability and propensity to learn anything at will. Therefore a learning concept is needed in educational science which, with regard to *what* is learned, is completely open, i.e., is not definitionally tied to any specific learning result. It must be applicable to *all* learning, regardless of what results are produced and how anyone evaluates these results.

Furthermore, a concept of learning usable by educational science must also be free of any reference to specific postulated learning conditions (as for example education). A concept such as "educationally steered socialization" is also questionable, because from the outset it definitionally ascribes specific positively evaluated learning results to a specific class of external stimuli, namely educational actions as the (chief) cause of these learning results. It is simply assumed in this concept of socialization that given learning results or the commencement of a learning process can be attributed to *one* among the various *possible* conditions. This condition is singled out, all other possible conditions are ignored, and the misconception is encouraged and spread that there is already sufficient validated knowledge of the nomological relationships between education and socialization to permit the one to be seen as the cause and the other as its effect.

The use of the expressions "socializand" and "socialization candidate"[252] also contributes to spreading this illusion. The substantive "socializand" (as a derivative from the Latin "socialisandus," analogical to "educandus") would only be meaningful if one assumed that there were such an activity as *Latin* "socialisare" ("to make social") so that by a "socializand" could be understood a "person to be made social," i.e., an object or addressee of "socializing" actions. However, since Rössner defines "socialization" as learning and *not* as educating (or "making social"), his use of the term "socializand" contradicts his concept of socialization. That he nevertheless employs it is of course in keeping with his failure to hold consistently to his concept of socialization, as he often uses the term "socialization" when he means "education." Thus, for example, we find him using the verb "to socialize" for "to educate," "socializationally weak" for "educationally weak," "socializing authorities" for "educational authorities," etc.[253] He even refers to "successful socialization" (in the sense of "successful education"),[254] although "socialization" in his sense (as learning) must *always* "succeed." This is because success is included in the definition, i.e., socialization is inferred from the appearance of a positively evaluated learning result.

Geulen

Dieter Geulen defines "socialization" "as a *process of the genesis of the personality in dependence on the environment* which, as we assume, is always historically and socially mediated" (I).[255] This concept of socialization is extremely poor in content and has accordingly a very broad extension. The term "socialization" refers in this case to no attributes beyond the "becoming of the personality." That this process occurs "in dependence on the environment" is not an additional specification, but is already included in the concept of the "genesis of the personality." Geulen rejects a "limitation of the concept of socialization to specific psychological mechanisms such as 'learning' or 'identification'," just as much as its limitation "to specific types of contents or personality attributes, such as to the domain of the 'values,' 'norms' or 'roles' obligatory in the relevant society."[256] No relationship to any meaning of the word "social," is to be found in this concept of socialization, since it dispenses not only with the conceptual attribute "socially relevant psychic dispositions" as the result of the process of socialization, but also with the attribute "social" in the sense of "learning in interaction with social partners."

Anyone who thinks that this is the broadest imaginable concept of socialization soon learns that Geulen actually favors a still broader one which he has, unfortunately, neglected to explicitly define. However, he unambiguously expresses a desire to limit the concept of socialization neither to "education" nor to "personal influences in the broadest sense": "the domain of unintended or unconscious influences," including those which emanate from the "object world," should not be "bracketed out." His statements make sense only if we assume that not just education and all "personal influences in the broadest sense" but also all influences emanating from the "objective world" fall under the concept of "socialization." "Socialization II" thus means for Geulen *the process of the genesis of the personality* (or the "genesis of the human subject"[257]) *and all environmental influences by which it is determined.*

Besides this Geulen also uses a third concept of socialization which, as in the case of the second, he does not explicitly introduce, but which can be fairly easily reconstructed. He writes of "socialization aims," of the "aims of socialization to whose realization the socialization scientist, through his work, wishes to contribute" and of the "subject to be socialized." He even asserts "that socialization aims are the actual objects of interest for a theory of socialization," at least for a so-called "critical socialization theory" such as he advocates.[258] We can only make sense of these statements if we understand "socialization" to mean not the "process of the genesis of the personality" (which can of course have no aim), but rather "education" (III). At many points, however, "socialization" seems also to mean "*political action*," for Geulen is above all interested in the "action-mediated relationship between socialization aims and societal change." Accordingly he emphasizes "that the aims of socialization and the dependent variables of a socialization theory can only arise from a utopian conception of society and an exact analysis of the necessary individual steps which lead from a contemporary state to a future one."[259]

Kob

Janpeter Kob asserts first that the concept of socialization "designates . . . a *diffuse and in principle undemarcatable processual interrelationship.*" Then, however, he defines "socialization" as "every *process in which*, through direct or indirect interactions, the *development* of relatively stable *behavioral dispositions comes about* in the individual person" (I). "Education" is designated as a "special case," as a "very particular variant of socialization." The concept of education isolates from the processes called "socialization" those "actions consciously aimed at influencing people in a stable fashion. . . . Thus understood, *education* is *a subconcept of socialization.*"[260]

"By the classical sociological category of socialization" is meant "*the conditions for the origin of a . . . social character,*" whereby what must be taken into account is "always *the sum total* of the respectively typical *factors* in the societal interrelationship," including those factors "*which determine the individual person,* those to which he is forced to adapt. . . . The field of these factors is in every case virtually unlimited." Simply because of the number of factors to be taken into account, it would be "an endless task to adequately describe the *total process of socialization* within a society. Just the attempt to undertake this for a single individual would require a total analysis of his society down to the particular individual structures in which he has lived and lives."[261]

Obviously we are already dealing here with two concepts of socialization. "Socialization I" means "every process in which . . . the development . . . of behavioral dispositions . . . in people comes about." From this statement it is unclear whether the author is referring to (a) (inner) learning processes or (b) (external) influencing processes or (c) a comprehensive process which includes both external influencing processes and the learning processes that they have set in motion or conditioned in the person influenced. From the context, in which the "*extra-individually* determined genesis of the 'social personality'" is discussed, we could perhaps assume that (external) influencing processes (Ib) might be intended.

One reason for rejecting this interpretation is Kob's statement that "in" the "process" called "socialization" the "development" of dispositions comes about "*through* direct or indirect interaction." The "development" of dispositions cannot possibly come about "through . . . interaction" occurring "in" an influencing process. By "interaction" we understand a reciprocal influencing process (whereby we need not discuss here the question of what could be meant by "indirect" interaction). If Kob really intended "socialization" to mean an "influencing process," the "process" called "socialization" would have to be seen as identical with a subset of these reciprocal influencing processes. This subset would comprehend that share of influencing processes which do not emanate from the individual thought to be determined by socialization, but which, to the contrary, determine him. It seems therefore that an inner learning process (Ia) is indeed meant.

However, this interpretation is put in question by the fact that Kob would then have defined "socialization" as a *learning process* "in which . . . the development" of dispositions comes about. This would only make sense if "development" is used here as in everyday language and means nothing other than "coming about" (or "formation"). If, however, a developmental process in a scientific sense is intended, this would mean that the totality of maturation and learning processes comes about in a subprocess of the developmental process (learning). Since this interpretation of the word "development" as meant in a scientific sense leads to an absurd conclusion, we must assume that in Kob's definition it is really being used in a non-scientific sense. Having made this assumption, nothing would prevent us from interpreting Kob's "Socialization I" as a "learning process," if we did not know from the context that he refers primarily to "extra-individual" factors and processes as conditions for the "development" of "behavioral dispositions in individual persons" and wishes to explicitly include "education" in "socialization." "Education," however, cannot possibly be understood as a "special case," as a "variant" or as a "subconcept" of "learning." Therefore we can rightly assume that Kob refers with "Socialization I" to "every process" "in which" through an external influencing process external "factors" effect a learning process giving rise to behavioral dispositions in a person (Ic).

This conceptual definition shows clearly that Kob's socialization concept I is not limited to processes leading to the development of a specific class of dispositions, such as "social" or "socially relevant" ones, but is applicable to every process through which the development of all possible "relatively stable behavioral dispositions . . . comes about." The only possible connection between this concept and the word "social" as a component of the term "socialization" consists in the fact that one could think of *social* interactions as also falling among the "interactions" through which dispositions arise.

A second concept, "Socialization II," is for Kob a "*total* process" or an "in principle *undemarcatable processual interrelationship*," one which cannot "be adequately described."[262] "Socialization is a central sociological category which designates a basic perspective of every sociological approach: *the social person and the socially conditioned nature of individual action.*"[263] While for Kob "Socialization I" is an extremely complex hypothetical construct, one which stands for a class of hypothetical processes, "Socialization II" designates only a "perspective of sociological theory,"[264] presumably in the sense of a viewpoint for examining societal phenomena.

Important for understanding Kob's attempted clarification of the relationship between "socialization and education" is his statement that "socialization" is not a designation for a "specific type of social action," while "education" is definitely a "special case of social action." It is impossible "to describe socialization as a closed system of action."[265] Thus according to Kob, on the one hand, "education is a subconcept of socialization," and on the other, it is a subconcept of the concept of "social action."[266] However, without introducing great limitations (to "*successful* social action" through which a specific object of action is "made social"), "social action" cannot be viewed as a subconcept of "socialization." This is because in any case "socialization" is an effect concept under which only *completed* actions could be subsumed, insofar as *it was proved* that these actions, as influencing processes, had brought about learning processes in one or more persons which had led to the creation of behavioral dispositions. Such a proof can understandably be attempted only *after the fact for a concrete case* of education, but not for the sum total of all phenomena falling under the concept of education. Therefore it is quite unrealistic to include as a conceptual attribute in the concept of education the appearance of intended effects (i.e., the success) of education. Anyone who formulates such a "success concept of education" should clearly understand that in the real world we would seldom encounter the conditions for its application. Practically and scientifically useful is only the "intentional concept of education," in which education is defined as action without regard to success.[267] In most cases this sense of the word "education" is also the one intended, both in everyday language and in pedagogical terminology.

Although Kob emphasizes that "socialization" should not be understood as social action, he writes of the "aim of socialization," the "aim of the socialization process" or "socialization aims" and of the "person to be socialized."[268] Since we can only speak meaningfully of an "aim" if a person exists who sets, establishes or has one (for an "aim" presupposes an intention), a process to which an aim is attributed can only be an action. Nor can one speak meaningfully of a "person to be socialized" unless an agent exists who should or wants to "socialize" that person, and if "to socialize" refers to action. Thus Kob has a third concept of socialization, "Socialization III," which means for him "*education*." He also calls this concept "educational socialization"[269] or "consciously steered socialization."[270]

However, Kob additionally writes of education as the "completion or correction of socialization."[271] Education is intended to "correct . . . socialization"[272] and is, in this case, a "continuation of other, mainly non-educational socialization."[273] At the same time, he asserts of both "educational" and "non-educational" socialization: "Both processes are structurally so different from one another that in principle they must be incommensurable."[274] The word "incommensurable" means "incapable of being measured" or "lacking a common quality upon which to make a comparison."[275] Of course it is correct to say that "Socialization I" and education are "structurally different" and "incommensurable." But still it remains inexplicable that someone who knows this nevertheless calls education a "special case," a "variant" or a "subconcept" of "socialization" and distinguishes between "non-educational" and "educational" socialization. If we take seriously Kob's claim that both are structurally different and incommensurable, we must accordingly assume that he employs still a fourth concept of socialization. Kob's "Socialization IV" can be characterized as *an influencing process which has not arisen from any intention to influence (or which is not education).*

Kob's fifth concept, "Socialization V," refers to *the result of the socialization process* or the state of "*being socialized.*" Thus, for example, Kob says that behavioral regularities are not primarily the intended results of "socialization" and that "socialization" is an "unintended side effect."[276]

"Socialization VI" is defined as follows: "The process of socialization is . . . *not only* . . . *a process* . . . *in which an individual is moulded* by his societal situation *into a social person capable of acting* in society, but also . . . *a permanent action of the individual* in which the latter 'makes something of himself'."[277] This concept is distinguished from "Socialization I" in two respects. First, the result of the process is stated to be the "*social person capable of acting.*" Second, besides the process of being "moulded by his societal situation," the conceptual attribute "permanent action of the individual" is also introduced. The word "permanent" means "fixed and changeless; lasting or meant to last indefinitely," "not expected to change in status, condition, or place."[278] It remains unclear what one should understand by a "permanent action" in which the individual "makes something of himself." If one takes the word "action" literally, then "permanent action" appears to be something that no one is capable of. It also remains completely unclear how the process of being moulded by the societal situation in the "process of socialization" relates to the "permanent action" of the individual in which "he makes something of himself." One would like to know whether the author means that through permanent action the individual makes of himself *that* into which he is "moulded" by his societal situation, or whether he makes something else of himself, since the individual is already "moulded by his societal situation into a social person capable of acting." More precise details about these matters are indispensable in order to be able to decide whether there are phenomena in the world which fall under this concept.

"Socialization VII" means "*the process of fundamental and steadily moulding social determination of each person and his individual development into a social person.*"[279] The content of this concept is alleged to be equivalent in sense to socialization understood "as the real '*second, socio-cultural birth' of the individual person.*"[280]

This concept differs from "Socialization VI" in that here the "process . . . of social determination" is not coupled with the "permanent action of the individual," but with his "development into a social person." A second difference consists in the fact that Kob VI does not specify how the individual acts, but simply affirms that he makes "something" of himself, while with Kob VII he develops into a "social person." Although they clearly employ different terms, Socialization VII is just as confusing as Socialization VI. Obviously there is a great difference between "action" and "development," but the relationship between a "process of social determination" and "development into a social person" referred to in "Socialization VII" is scarcely clearer than that which exists between the process of being "moulded by his societal situation" and the "permanent action" through which the individual "makes something of himself" referred to in "Socialization VI." Understanding is also hindered by the fact that Kob does not explain the essential conceptual attribute "to mould" or "moulding." "To mould" is an ambiguous word.[281] When he speaks of "steadily moulding social determination" Kob is, at any rate, offering a collection of expressions for the person's moulding by societal factors. This makes sense at most if "development into a social person" is not merely viewed as in some sense externally linked to this social determination, but is understood as the central process intended by the socialization concept, and if the first half of the definition is interpreted as simply an unclear designation for the societal subconditions or determinants (as a share of all determinants) of this developmental process. But since "steadily moulding social determination" is something other than "social determinants," the wording of Kob's definition makes his concept "Socialization VII" unclear.

The characterization of *socialization as the "second, socio-cultural birth of the person"* derives from a metaphor popularized by René König.[282] While this sense is frequently employed and is even regarded by many authors as a scientific concept,[283] in fact the expression is based on a false analogy.[284] The word "birth" refers to the delivery of a child, thus to an observable event of short duration. "Socialization," to the contrary—regardless of how we define it—is a non-observable hypothetical process to which long duration is ascribed: in the most extreme case lifelong, in the case of so-called "primary socialization," at least six to ten years. A "second birth" extending over several years is hard to imagine, quite apart from the fact that, in the case of "socio-cultural birth," it remains completely unclear what the core meaning could be which this process has in common with childbirth. One could of course interpret birth as a person's entry into the social world, but this has already occurred in the single real, "first" birth. What König and those who have uncritically adopted his metaphor really mean is the "construction of the socio-cultural personality" through "moral education," "elementary education" or "social structuring of the person,"[285] which have nothing to do with birth. This is clear if one replaces the word "birth" with the synonym "delivery." A "second, socio-cultural delivery of the person" makes no sense, because "delivery" means leaving the womb, while the users of the thoughtlessly employed metaphor of a person's "second birth"[286] are trying to express just the opposite: a person's becoming bound to or integrated into a socio-cultural environment with its norms.

Heinz

According to Walter Heinz, "socialization" means "quite generally *the transformation of the biological into a social being* with specific cultural standards for interpreting reality" (I). "Transformation" is not only vague, it is also an ambiguous term. It can mean *i.* an act of transforming; *ii.* a mere process in whose course something assumes a different form without an actor having tried to and succeeded in bringing this about; *iii.* the result respectively of an action in sense *i.* or of a process in sense *ii.* Meanings *i.* and *ii.* are both ambiguous: An act of transformation can be reflexive ("self-transformation") or transitive ("transforming another"). The process could likewise be one occurring in a self-transforming subject or an external influencing process through which an object is transformed.

Appropriate for this ambiguity is that Heinz, on the one hand, defines "socialization as a *process of adaptation*," as "the individual's *finding a footing in* societal structural and interactional contexts," "as *a process of social learning*" (II). On the other, he means by "socialization" the "*process of passing on culture* to the respectively younger generation," "the *transmission* of guiding ideals, values and norms to children and adolescents," the "organized, *conscious socialization activity* of educators" (III).[287] He speaks of "socialization organized by the schools" and of the "increasingly scientific nature and professionalization even of privately organized socialization processes."[288] Even if we ignore the fact that not socialization processes, but at most only educators ("socializers") and particularly their training can "professionalize" or confer a "scientific nature," in this case the word "socialization" still means nothing more than education.

Socialization III can be understood as one of the conditions for Socialization II. Socialization II and III can be combined in Socialization I. In this sense Heinz assigns to the object of socialization research "everything which relates to . . . social learning processes, their conditions and consequences."[289]

Knoll

Jörg Knoll understands "socialization *as a process function consisting of persons, the social environment and their interactions.*"[290] He points to the "complexity of socialization" and recommends "relating socialization to all processes of the person's *becoming social. Education* is also included in this."[291]

Although a "process function" can have no aims, Knoll attributes "*aims*" to the "process of socialization" and mentions as such "interaction ability," subdivided into "behavioral qualifications . . . which are necessary and which make it possible to relate oneself to others and others to oneself (identification), to realize this reciprocal relationship (interaction and communication), to recognize it as such and to reflect it (meta-communication)."[292]

Hurrelmann

Klaus Hurrelmann writes of "*socializing and educating processes,*" of "societally planned and organized socialization and education."[293] Since following Geulen he defines socialization as the "process of the *genesis of the personality,*"[294] one is faced by the question of what a "societally planned and organized genesis of the personality" would be like. Certainly it is no concept for empirical science but at most one for utopian thinking.

Perhaps the formula "socializing and educating processes" can be understood to mean "influencing and educating processes," for in another passage Hurrelmann re-

fers to "socializing processes" as "influencing processes."[295] In favor of this interpretation is also the fact that
Hurrelmann views "socialization" as a "higher-level concept for education." This would be absurd if "socialization" meant here "genesis of the personality."

However, also possible is that the formula "socializing
and educating processes" merely expresses one and the
same concept with two different but synonymous words.
The formula would then be interpretable as follows: "*educating* and educating processes." Another thing which favors this interpretation is that Hurrelmann uses the
terms "educational aim" and "socialization aim" synonymously.[296] One must assume from this that the words
"education" and "socialization" are synonymous in his
thinking.

It does, to be sure, remain incomprehensible why
Hurrelmann assumes that besides "intentional and planned educational aims" there also exist "latent," "unintended and unplanned educational aims."[297] Such "aims"
cannot possibly exist, because they have never been "intended" by anyone, i.e., willed, set or established.[298]

Likewise his expression "*compensatory socialization*"
only makes sense if one presupposes that in this case
the term "socialization" means "education" and not—as
Hurrelmann defines it—the "process of the genesis of the
personality." What could one then imagine a "compensatory genesis of the personality" to be?

As well with this text the reader is thus forced to infer
the protean meanings with which the author employs his
"broadly conceived interdisciplinary . . . higher-level concept"[299] of "socialization."

We have now determined what twenty-four representative authors understand "socialization" to mean. The
texts we have examined stem from three decades and
contain all the essential meanings related to this term in
the social sciences. Taken together, these meanings comprehend a vast range of real and hypothetical objects of
manifold nature. There is no way in which a concept of
socialization representing the sum total of all these het-

erogeneous meanings could be scientifically fruitful.[300] Concepts should demarcate things which belong together from everything else and help distinguish those which are different from one another. If no specification is made, we have the confusing, most general concept of socialization, which fails to demarcate and differentiate, but instead arbitrarily combines aspects which do not really belong together. The concept is so vague that it remains unclear "what factual contents, themes and theories really do *not* belong to the subject matter of socialization theory."[301] Its use is an indication that in socialization research "lack of theories, inadequate analytical precision and naivety in the formulation of hypotheses" are widespread.[302]

Is it possible to give this vague concept a more precise meaning?[303] Certainly not, if we attempt to include in the concept *all* the attributes with which we have become acquainted in our semantic analysis. We can achieve a scientifically useful concept of socialization only by making a *selection* from the existing senses of the word "socialization." For this purpose a logically consistent and realistic combination of attributes would have to be selected. What socialization concepts are available as a basis for this selection?

THE CLASSIFICATION OF PERSON-RELATED CONCEPTS OF SOCIALIZATION

It is worthwhile to first distinguish between (a) process concepts and (b) product concepts of socialization. Product concepts, which refer to the result, effect, outcome or product of a process ("socialization" as a person's psychic state or dispositional network), are relatively rare and their discussion will be put off until later in this text.

Process Concepts of Socialization

Common to most socialization concepts is the attribute "process." The word "*process*" comes from the Latin "procedere," meaning "to go forward, advance," and was formed by combining "pro," meaning "before, in front of" with "cedere," meaning "to go." A process is a "system of operations in the production of something," a "series of actions, changes, or functions that bring about an end or result," the "course or passage of time," "ongoing movement, progression,"[304] "continuous change,"[305] "connected, regularly proceeding operation,"[306] a "dynamic sequence of various states of a thing or system."[307] "*Process*" can also mean "something which is occurring," such as a presently "occurring event." "To occur" means to "take place; come about," "be found to exist or appear."[308]

The antonym of "process" is "state."[309] If "socialization" is defined as a "process," one still knows nothing more than that it means a "progression," "ongoing movement" or *a course of events occurring over time*,[310] as opposed to a state, i.e., a "condition of being in a stage or form, as of structure."[311] One must accordingly ask: through what features does a process called "socialization" differ from all other processes?

The differences among socialization concepts are a matter, first, of *the type of process* respectively intended, and, second, of *the results* of these different processes. The most important distinction in regard to types of processes is between *inner processes* which take place *within the person* and whose subject or bearer is the person affected (intra-personal or intra-subjective process), and *external processes* which occur *in the environment* of the person who is affected and who is their object.

Socialization as an Intra-Personal Process

Intra-personal processes can be classified as organic (or physical), psychic and psycho-physical. Regarded as organic processes are growth, maturation and development in a narrower biological sense. To be sure there is no agreement about the meaning of these terms and their mutual demarcation.[312] The psychic processes which come into consideration in defining socialization concepts are processes of learning. Learning processes are, however, frequently conceived of as psycho-physical processes, because it is assumed that they have an organic (neural) basis.

In addition, there is a concept of development understood as a psycho-physical process, as well as one referring to strictly psychic processes. Viewed as essential for all three types, organic, psycho-physical and psychic "development," is that they involve "an irreversible process which occurs only once in time," one of "becoming more specific," of "change in form and functions" which culminates in an end state and is chiefly "determined by inner laws of the organism" contained in hereditary predispositions.[313] In a, to be sure, less precise sense one sometimes also speaks of "development" when mere change is meant. If one wishes to get around the insoluble problem of what share maturation and learning processes have in the emergence of psychic dispositions, one may even use the broadest of all developmental concepts, that of "becoming."[314]

Socialization as the Becoming of Personality

A relatively small group of authors understands "socialization" as the process of the personality's becoming. It is referred to with the expressions "development" (Parsons II, Zigler/Child, Roth), "process of change" (Secord/Backman), "ontogenetic process" (Berger/Luckmann) and "genesis of the personality"[315] (Geulen I). None of the authors who speak of "development" in this regard thereby intends the biological sense of the word. It appears rather that they mean a superordinated process involving not only developmental (in the biological sense), but also learning processes.

The cited authors differ in their views about the results of "socialization." Some understand "socialization" as the process of becoming of the "*total* personality" (Geulen, Hurrelmann). Most, however, delimit the process to the becoming of the "*social* personality" or of the psychic dispositions relevant to social life.

Socialization as a Learning Process

By far the greatest number of authors understand social-ization as a learning process or a sum of learning pro-cesses (Parsons I, Elkin, Brim I, Clausen, Inkeles III, Secord/Backman I, Claessens II, Neidhardt II, Haber-mas, Fend I, Mollenhauer, Roth I, Kuckartz II, Fröhlich, Rössner, Heinz II).

Some of these authors refer to the respective learning process as "*social* learning" (Clausen, Heinz II), "socially relevant learning" (Inkeles III, Rössner) or "socially spe-cific learning" (Rössner). These expressions have various meanings depending on whether the adjective "social" re-fers to external subconditions (causes) or to the results (effects) of learning. Some authors use them in the sense of learning conditioned by interaction with social part-ners (Secord/Backman I); others intend learning which leads to socially relevant learning results "which are eval-uated by societal authorities" or "judged to fulfill their norms" (Rössner).

There are great differences among statements about the *results* of socialization, i.e., about the psychic dispo-sitions whose creation through hypothetical learning processes the authors attempt to explain. The range ex-tends from psychic dispositions for "socially relevant be-havior and experience" (Zigler/Child, Fröhlich) to dispo-sitions for behavior which groups approve of and which accord with group members' expectations (Parsons I, Habermas, Secord/Backman) or are consistent with soci-ety's dominant behavioral norms (Neidhardt II). Above all extremely complex dispositional networks are named which are identical with the *personality as a whole*: the ability "to function within a given society" (Elkin); to be "more or less able members of their society" (Brim I);[316] social "action ability" (Habermas);[317] "qualifications" which enable one to "communicate" with social partners (Mollenhauer). In addition to these, dispositional net-works are also named which can be thought of as as-pects of the personality: the ability to act in ways appro-priate for societal roles (Parsons I, Habermas); the disposition to behave in accord with societally legitimate valuations and norms (Fend I).

There is only a minor difference between "socialization as the becoming of the personality" and "socialization as a learning process." It consists in the fact that with the first concept there is no limitation to learning processes, but also maturation and developmental processes are included as parts of the total process, while these are excluded with the second concept. Since both concepts draw on hypothetical processes which are not observable in reality and therefore cannot be differentiated from one another, the difference between them is inessential. As far as the *results* of both constructed processes are concerned, there is no difference.

If both concepts are subsumed under the concept of "socialization as an intra-personal process," we can clearly see that in most conceptual definitions found in sociological and psychological literature dealing comprehensively with socialization, *this* concept is the one intended.

Socialization as a Socio-Cultural Influencing Process

This concept means a process (or sum of processes) in the person's environment assumed to influence the hypothetical intra-personal learning process that creates the "total personality" or the "social personality." The external influencing process is viewed as a (partial) condition for the inner learning process and thereby also for its learning results. Strictly speaking this influencing process is just as much a hypothetical process as is that of learning. It is postulated on the assumption that specific environmental conditions so influence people that they are transformed from plastic, still indeterminate organisms into "personalities" or from "not yet social personalities" into "social personalities."

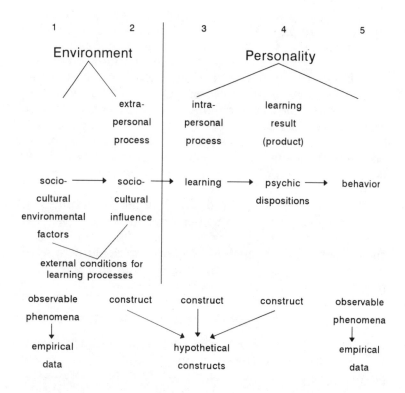

Causal Scheme "Socialization"

With this socialization concept most authors accentu-
ate a certain subset of the entire range of influencing
processes to which people are exposed in their environments. This subset consists of influences emanating
from people and their works (objectivations, culture)
(Zigler/Child, Brim II, Wurzbacher, Kob I, Kob IV,
Neidhardt III, Fend II, Kuckartz I). The authors of some
texts, however, occasionally write of "environmental conditions" in general, which they assume are always "to be

viewed as socially mediated."[318]

The concept of socialization as an influencing process has the essential attribute that learning results actually appear in the persons subject to this process. The occurrence of socialization in this sense is thus inferred from its effects. Only if a psychic disposition (or dispositional constellation) inferred from behavior and thought to have resulted from learning is *demonstrably* a *result* of an environmental factor *x* can an influencing process referred to as "socialization" be assumed to have occurred and to have been (partially) produced by this factor. We have here a relationship similar to that which exists between a psychic disposition (ability, attitude, knowledge, etc.) interpreted as a learning result and the hypothetical learning process assumed to be the cause of this result. Actually observable are only the first and last links of the five-step chain "socio-cultural environmental factors—socio-cultural influencing process—learning process—psychic disposition as learning result—behavior." The intermediate steps are hypothetical constructs.

Given its hypothetical nature, we see clearly that the concept of "socialization as an influencing process" can strictly speaking only be employed *retrospectively* in reference to an already completed process. Inkeles (II) alone has offered a definition appropriate to this aspect: "socialization" is "the sum total of *past* experiences an individual has had."[319]

Some of the authors who intend "socialization" to mean an influencing process say explicitly that this concept includes that of education (Kuckartz I, Kob I, Hurrelmann). For this to be possible a concept of education must be presupposed which has all the attributes of the concept "socialization as an influencing process." Accordingly "education" can here only mean a past social influencing process which can be shown to have actually produced the effect it is claimed to have caused. Thus we have an effect concept of education which is in practice unusable. Proof that a realized effect was caused by a process termed "education"—which would have to be specified more precisely—can only rarely be obtained, and then at most only after the fact.[320]

The described *results* of "socialization as an influencing process" are no different from those of "socialization as a learning process." This cannot be otherwise, for both concepts are constructed on the basis of the same results and differ only in that one refers to the second (extra-personal) and the other the third (intra-personal) member of the five-link hypothetical causal chain presented above.

Socialization as a Combination of Extra-Personal and Intra-Personal Processes

This concept of socialization refers to an overall process thought of as combining extra-personal and intra-personal processes. In its relatively simplest form it has as its contents the sum of all extra-personal socio-cultural influencing processes and of all intra-personal learning processes assumed to be conditions for the emergence of the personality as a whole or of its societally relevant dispositions. Expressed differently: the concept comprehends a complex of the most proximate inner conditions (learning processes) and the most distant external conditions (influencing processes) for the creation of the personality, and specifically for the creation of societally relevant psychic dispositions. Since this process could not even be defined without specifying its result, the latter constitutes an essential conceptual attribute. In terms of our five-step causal scheme, this concept of socialization comprehends the second, third and fourth steps. We find this socialization concept in Inkeles I, Claessens I and Neidhardt I.

Other authors also explicitly expand the concept of socialization to include socio-cultural environmental factors or all environmental factors seen as conditions for the influencing process (and thereby at the same time for the overall process). Thus in these cases the first link of the hypothetical causal chain is included in the conceptual definition. The broadest concept of this type is Geulen II: "socialization" refers in this definition to "the genesis of the personality" and all environmental influences through which it is conditioned. But Claessens I, Kob VII, Heinz I and Knoll can also be interpreted in this sense.

There is no essential difference between the two conceptual variants of socialization as a combination of extra- and intra-personal processes. They agree in referring to a process including its conditions and effects.

The most complex special forms of the combined extra- and intra-personal concept of socialization are those in which educational actions are also included among the extra-personal processes (Clausen, Goslin). Since only processes which in fact are (partial) conditions or (partial) causes of "socialization" effects fall within the scope of these concepts, only an effect concept of education is logically acceptable in this conceptual framework. However, the authors ignore the fundamental difference between intentional and effect concepts of education. They employ the intentional concept of education naively, taking into account neither educational failure nor the difficulties involved in proving educational success. Such proof presupposes, among other things, that for research purposes education can be methodically *isolated* from all non-educational influencing processes and will *not* be lost from sight, merged inseparably with the sum total of all relevant influencing processes and their conditions. But, to the contrary, the conflation of education and influencing processes is unavoidable with this concept of socialization.

As to the results of the total process referred to by this concept, there is no difference between it and other concepts of socialization which we have already dealt with above. These results extend, as usual, from "being social" (Knoll), the "person capable of acting socially" (Kob VI) or the "social being" (Heinz I) to "behavioral dispositions" (Neidhardt I) and to the presence in the mind of "socio-cultural contents," "values" and "culture" (Claessens).

Socialization as Education

By education we mean actions through which persons attempt to in some manner permanently improve other person's networks of psychic dispositions, to preserve the components judged valuable or to prevent the emergence of dispositions judged to be bad.[321]

Those authors who use the term "socialization" for this concept circumscribe their meaning not only with the word "education," but also with the following words: "child rearing,"[322] training," "guiding" to learning, "punishing" and "rewarding" (Child); "teaching," "instructing" (Brim III); "forming and educating" (Claessens III); "transmitting" or "transferring" and "making" values, norms and life techniques "binding" (Neidhardt IIIe); "making social" (Fend III); "social education" (Roth IIIb); "educational socialization," "consciously steered socialization" (Kob III); "conscious socialization activity" (Heinz III).

Few details are given by these authors concerning the *results* which educators attempt to achieve in educands by means of "socialization understood as education." By and large, however, they coincide with those given for the socialization concepts already dealt with above. They extend from extremely indefinite specifications such as "actual behavior" (Child) to somewhat more exact ones such as the ability "to fulfill social obligations" (Inkeles IV).

Product Concepts of Socialization

The content of a product concept of socialization is a network of psychic dispositions viewed as the effect or result (Inkeles I) of the socialization process: the "social being," the "socialized person" or the "state of having been socialized." Socialization concepts of this sort are encountered relatively infrequently in scientific literature (besides Inkeles I also in Berger/Luckmann, Claessens IV, Roth IV, Kob IV).

Similar to the word "education" in the sense of a state of "having an education" or of "being an educated person,"[323] which can refer either to the state of an actual person or an educational ideal for a person, the expression "socialization as a product" could mean two things: first, the *real* psychic constitution of a person who has been "socialized" (e.g., Lochner: "socialization as a result"[324]); or second, the *ideal* of a psychic constitution which a person ought to realize (Lochner: "socialization as an aim";[325] Berger/Luckmann: "Socialization is never total and never finished"[326]).

My attempt to clarify and classify the person-related sociological, psychological and pedagogical meanings of the word "socialization" has shown that there are essentially four different process senses plus the product sense. Beyond this, however, the four process concepts are often also combined into a cloudy overall concept, one whose critique has been the starting point of this text. Thus it forms a fifth process concept, which can be referred to as the *"omnium-gatherum concept of socialization."* What good are the various concepts discussed above for establishing and communicating new insights? How are they to be judged?

EVALUATION OF SOCIALIZATION CONCEPTS

It can be said with certainty that the ambiguous and vague *omnium-gatherum concept of socialization* interferes with both the search for scientific knowledge and mutual understanding. It has arisen from sloppy thinking and is—where employed—a sign of sloppy thinking, because it conflates things which do not belong together. Therefore it is not even adequate as a general orientational aid, but only spreads confusion. Anyone who wants to think and speak clearly should not use it.

Is there one among the other four remaining process concepts of socialization which is sufficiently clear and theoretically fruitful to deserve being favored? Conceptual confusion cannot be overcome as long as at least four different concepts of socialization continue to be employed simultaneously and at cross-purposes. Are *all* of them unusable or is there one which could serve us better than the others?

There are three criteria which may help us in judging.
i. Non-Redundancy: A concept which is already used under another name need not be referred to by the term
"socialization." *ii.* Empirical Content: What empirical
facts (empirical findings, data) speak in favor of or
against a concept? *iii.* Logical Adequacy: A concept
should be precise and consistent with a system of interrelated concepts already present for the subject area. We
will test the remaining process concepts of socialization
on the basis of these criteria.

Critique of the Meaning "Socialization as Education"

Anyone who says "socialization" and means "education"
has a clear concept neither of socialization nor of education, for the basic sense of "socialization" is quite different from that of "education." Therefore no concept of socialization, however clearly defined, can replace the concept of education or serve as its higher-level concept.
While to be sure there is more than one concept of education, nevertheless "*to educate*" has for all peoples in all
historical periods referred to "*aim-oriented action.*" "Education"—put simply—is understood to mean actions
through which people attempt to in some respect further
the personalities of other persons.[327]

Identifying the essential attribute of a precise concept
of education as action implies that education includes
aims, intentions, an attempt character and uncertainty
about results. "To educate" is a task or attempt verb, not
a success verb.[328] A useful concept of education refers to
the actor's intention, not to the effect which his action
produces. Education is always a means of achieving intended ends, but it always remains definitionally open
whether the intended results are or can in fact be realized. The concept of education is an empirical concept
which includes evaluations and volitional experiences
and is thought of in terms of the *end-means schema.*[329] It
focuses on means, which are called "educational actions."

In contrast to education, the *concept of socialization* is conceived of in terms of the *causal* or *cause-and-effect schema*, however, in the reverse order: starting from an effect it focuses on the sum of the processes through which this effect has been brought about or conditioned. Socialization is a postulated process, a purely hypothetical mental construction. All person-related concepts of socialization are theoretical constructs, not empirical concepts. They thereby serve to designate an unknown complex of processes leading with causal necessity to very imprecisely specified effects. As hypothetical causal concepts lacking informational content, they are explanatory concepts without explanatory value.

Obviously one can assume that among the conditions for the creation of a person's societally relevant characteristics are educational actions directed by others at that person. However, it would be extremely naive to regard "social character" as solely the result of the educational actions to which people have been exposed. Educational actions make up only a share of the external conditions under which social character emerges. In no case can we determine with certainty what they have concretely brought about and in what manner.

Since the concept of education is indispensable and is generally used under this name, there is no good reason for also calling it "socialization." Those who nevertheless do so should know that they are thereby violating accepted rules of usage and, at any rate, are speaking of an entirely different matter than the process by which the "social" personality arises, a process for whose designation the word "socialization" was introduced. There is no way to combine both meanings (education and the becoming of the "social personality") in an empirically adequate and logically unobjectionable concept. The use of a socialization concept which conflates educational action with non-aim-directed causal processes shows a lack of clarity concerning both.

Unfortunately this is far too often the case. It seldom happens that authors employ the terms "socialization" and "to socialize" *exclusively* as new names for the con-

cept of education. Instead they almost always understand the concept of socialization to include, besides
education, processes which do *not* fall under the concept
of education, but are of an entirely different sort. Usually
the non-educational sense even forms the central contents of "omnium-gatherum" concepts. Created through
category errors, such concepts cannot be precisely defined. They must, rather, be exposed and fought in their
ambiguity, unrealistic character and contradictoriness.

Objections to the Remaining Senses

Having rejected as superfluous and misleading the concept of "socialization understood as education," three
chief senses remain, all of which are mutually incompatible. One must decide whether "socialization" is to mean
an *intra*-personal, *extra*-personal or *combined* process.
Since nothing is gained if everyone chooses a different
concept, achieving consensus is essential. There is, however, still another possibility: all three remaining concepts of socialization could be unusable. The consensus
would then have to be: Reject the term "socialization" in
all its person-related senses!

In order to reach a decision, it suffices to start from
the simplest of the three concepts and concentrate thereby on the attributes which it has in common with the
other two. The simplest is the concept of "socialization as
an intra-personal process." The common attributes are:
sum of processes through which people acquire the psychic dispositions for social experience and behavior in
harmony with the specific culture of their group (abbrevi-
ated: "social action ability"). This refers to a process *within the person* assumed to be the condition for the emergence of social action ability. The second concept, "socialization as a socio-cultural influencing process," refers
to the sum of the processes *in the person's environment*
which are assumed to be the *external* conditions for the
genesis of those intra-personal processes forming the
content of the first socialization concept. The third and
most complicated process concept of socialization com-

prehends the sum of the two sets of processes referred to by the first and second process concepts. Since these three concepts refer to different views of one and the same causal process, we can reasonably evaluate them together.

Common to all three is their reference to a hypothetical process of enormous complexity unified by a single attribute: a personality state quite vaguely characterized as the "social personality" or "social action ability." In each case "socialization" means no more than the sum total or the intra- and extra-personal processes which causally contribute to the emergence of the "social personality."

Critique of the Conceptual Attribute "Social Personality"

Since the "social personality" provided the occasion for formulating the concept of "socialization," and since it is the conceptual attribute which logically precedes the attribute "process" (i.e., the process is inferred from the social personality), I will begin with a critique of this attribute.

The "social" personality or "the personality capable of social action" is a concept comprehending an enormously complex dispositional network, one which is constantly changing and must accordingly be conceived of as dynamic rather than static. When is the "social" or "socialized" constitution of the personality finally achieved? What qualities must be present? What behavior identifies it? Only if there are empirically meaningful answers to these questions is it logically justified to subsume under the concept of socialization the sum of processes which one believes to have created the "personality capable of social action." Since this concept has been formed on the basis of the notion of a personality constitution thought to result from these processes, clarity is needed as to the attributes of the social personality. Otherwise the concept of socialization itself will be empty and theoretically useless.

One searches in vain for this clarity. There are only formal and extremely general specifications. Nothing else is possible with a concept intended to be universally applicable to all people. Real people have no general social action ability, but only particular attributes corresponding to specific demands which must be fulfilled in their socio-cultural situations. The attributes of the "social personality" thus differ from group to group and person to person.

Realistic consideration must, however, go further. We are by nature both persons and social beings. It would hardly be possible to empirically demarcate a "social" part of the personality from a "non-social." Rather it appears that the sum of peoples' "psychic dispositions for social experience and behavior" is identical with their personalities. Presumably it is this consideration which has moved some recent authors to, without including more detailed specifications, define "socialization" as the "becoming of personality."

One must note that this definition contains no substantive attributes, thus no references to a specific social personality constitution. Also lacking is the notion of a point in the course of human life at which this specific ("social") personality constitution is achieved. Its achievement would naturally signal the end of the hypothetical process through which it emerged. Socialization theorists have, to be sure, often asserted that socialization is a lifelong process, but this is logically inconsistent as long as this process is defined on the basis of a result achieved before the end of a person's lifetime.

If the personality thus remains substantively undefined, then obviously one can at every moment in life employ a concept of the sum of all previously occurring processes which have conditioned it. There is, however, no sensible reason for giving this concept the name "socialization." Since the concept has no specific "social" constitution of the personality as the name-giving chief attribute, it is senseless to designate with the word "social" the sum of processes thought of as causing the respective personality state. The appropriate name is rather

"the becoming of the personality" or—more problematically—"personality development" in a vague sense of the
word "development."

Critique of the Conceptual Attribute "Sum of All (Personality Determining) Processes"

Designated as "socialization" are not observable, but rather hypothetical, postulated processes. Not single processes, they are complex overall processes conceived of
as composed or constructed in an unspecified manner
from a great variety of unknown single processes. The
vocabulary of socialization has nothing to do with the observable world of the senses, but belongs rather to the
realm of hypotheses, the constructed world of postulated
objects and invented entities.

This is due to the fact that socialization theorists have
been prone to give a naive answer to a sensible but difficult question. The question is: how do the personality
qualities arise which enable people to live together with
others and help to perpetuate their society's culture? It
can be assumed that many qualities are necessary for
this and that each is conditioned by a variety of factors.
At any rate, the question can only be answered in small
steps through exhaustive research aided by realistic concepts. Such concepts as maturation, learning, example,
imitation, reward, punishment, social interaction, education, etc. have long been available. Instead of working
with them, however, social scientists have invented the
new concept of socialization. Thereby the false conception is favored that there is an identifiable process which
brings about societally relevant personality qualities. It
has been unwisely forgotten or never considered that the
concept of socialization simply refers to a mental construct: the sum of all causal processes which have contributed to the emergence of the whole constellation of
these personality qualities.

Such theoretical concepts can naturally be developed
starting from any personality quality, but they are very
impractical and misleading. They are impractical, be-

cause definitional logic restricts their application—strictly speaking—to a causal process which has already led to the relevant quality and thus is already complete and finished. They are misleading, because they veil ignorance with pseudo-knowledge and false conceptions of the personality, its emergence and change.

It is a mistake to postulate characteristic-specific processes as causes for the emergence of specific qualities and to think of them as real phenomena, distinguishable from processes which cause the emergence of other qualities. In this manner authors have, besides "socialization," also invented the processes of "individualization," "enculturation,"[330] "personalization,"[331] "moralization"[332] and "adultation."[333] One could in the same manner invent process terms for qualities which enable people to perform a variety of socio-cultural tasks. Some examples of such invented process terms could be: "lingualization"[334] (the development of linguistic competence), "professionalization"[335] (the development in a person of professional ability), "religiozation"[336] (the development of religious dispositions), "musicalization"[337] (the development of musical talents), "sexualization"[338] (the development of sex-specific dispositions), etc. In essence this has already occurred with the introduction of the concepts of "language socialization," "professional socialization," "religious socialization," "musical socialization" and "sex-role socialization,"[339] etc. Unfortunately this has added absolutely nothing to our knowledge of the real world.

To be able to think realistically about socialization, we must have a clear conceptual distinction between personality constitutions (states or qualities) and the various conditions for their emergence. A comprehensive process concept containing a specific result as a conceptual attribute is of necessity only applicable to the sum of all hypothetical processes which can be assumed to produce this result. Because the concept of socialization is defined on the basis of extremely complex results, one cannot possibly designate its actual temporally limited and very effect-specific subprocesses. Therefore it is no accident that authors usually write of the "socialization process" in the singular and portray it as a "lifelong" process. Compare this to the concept of learning, which is, to be sure, also a theoretical concept, but one universally applicable, because it is not defined in terms of specific learning results.

Critique of the Reinterpretation
of a Causal Process Concept
as a Teleological Action Concept

Person-related concepts of socialization are causal concepts which designate highly complicated causal processes. Their sense is, however, in most cases not consistently held to. Without being aware of it, authors often supplement or replace their attributes with ones belonging to the concept of action. Perhaps one reason for this is that in the political-economy sense (meaning "to nationalize," "to place under government or group ownership or control"[340]), "to socialize" is an action concept. Above all, however, people seem to have difficulty imagining the "social becoming" of the personality without drawing on actions performed with the intent to "make" the personality "social." This is why the confusion of socialization with education is so widespread.

In what manner does this confusion arise? An empirical fact, man's "social being," is reinterpreted from a mere result into the result of an action. It is understood not as an empirical fact resulting from the interaction of many (largely) unknown conditions, but is viewed instead as the realization of an aim.[341] Since aims can be set arbitrarily, it is assumed that the "social personality" could also be differently constituted if it were differently planned and brought into being through the application of the appropriate means. Thus the value-neutral descriptive concept of "social being" is imprudently transformed into an ideal, and causal processes are transformed into intentional actions. The emergence of the "social personality" is reinterpreted as an intentionally aim-guided process which, while accompanied by a few unpredictable and non-influenceable events, is by and large brought about purposefully.

This reinterpretation is made easier because it is not apparent from the process itself—in our case the becoming of the "social personality"—whether and to what extent it is (finally or teleologically) determined by the setting of ends and the employment of means. If people are involved it is hard to determine whether intentional actions or unintentional influences are at work. When one does not know whether aims have been set or means chosen, every effect can also be interpreted as intended, every cause as a means[342] to achieve an end or aim. Final interpretations are more attractive to simplistic minds than critical causal analysis or the admission of ignorance concerning the manner in which a phenomenon has arisen. Through their own aim-directed action people know the final form of determination best, and they tend to "assimilate everything unknown and unknowable to the well-known and usual."[343] As a consequence they are tempted to draw on an analogy with the purposefulness of the "social being" and view the socialization process as involving purposeful action, or even to interpret it as an entirely purposeful activity. Various "purposes" come in question: the fulfillment of "developmental tasks,"[344] the pursuit of "developmental aims"[345] or education to create a "social being."

Popular usage also favors this misinterpretation. As was mentioned above, the word "socialization" can mean not only an act of "making social," but also a process of "becoming social."[346] Each of these two senses designates a different range of phenomena, and various sorts of problems must be solved in order to understand them. Naming the various senses with the same word encourages uncritical thinkers to ignore significant differences and subsume them under a *single* concept.

Already conceptually this has ensured that, in using the socialization theory built upon this concept, unintended causal processes are constantly mistaken for purposeful, aim-oriented action. Strict causal analysis of self-contained processes through which the personality emerges become suffused with entirely different considerations directed at a systematic, planful future improvement of people and societies. There can be no intrinsic objection to dealing with such considerations in an educational theory framework. Nevertheless, knowledge of the conditions for the emergence of personality, however necessary for educational planning, can hardly be increased as long as causal relationships are confused with end-means relationships.[347] But precisely this mistake has become widespread through the arbitrary reinterpretation of the causal process concept of socialization as a teleological action concept.[348] Inadequacies in concept formation have contributed greatly to the result that socialization theories remain superficial and confused.

Conclusions and Recommendations

The emergence of the personality is one of the most complicated processes that exist. It began to be studied long before socialization vocabulary became fashionable, and it continues to be a central topic of the human sciences. However, at the conceptual level the processes connected with it deserve to be more sharply differentiated and precisely designated with terms less ambiguous and vague than "socialization." This term has, rather, given rise to unnecessary and basically superficial problems of understanding and communication instead of helping us to formulate and solve substantive problems.

In view of the conceptual confusion described above, I doubt whether terminological clarity can be attained in this area without completely rejecting the word "socialization." Therefore the best suggestion I can make is to simply stop using the term. It deserves to take a place among the many other obsolete terms which science has abandoned in the course of time.

However, since far beyond the circle of social scientists there are countless people who have become accustomed to using this term without an awareness of its problematic nature, it is unlikely that this will happen. Therefore I suggest as a provisional solution the following agreements:

a. The word "socialization" should be reserved as a term for the following concept: "the sum of learning processes through which people acquire the psychic dispositions for societal experience and behavior in accord with the norms specific to the culture of their groups" (or "societal action capability" or something similar).[349]

b. The socio-cultural environmental factors and influencing processes which are assumed to be the causes (or subcauses) of so-defined "socialization" should be called "socialization conditions."[350]

This means a choice in favor of the first of the three remaining process concepts of socialization: socialization as an intra-personal process, or more precisely as a learning process. This concept of socialization is relatively clear and agrees with the usage most often found in scientific texts. Nevertheless, it still does not change the fact that the concept is theoretically unfruitful and therefore dispensable for science. The term "socialization" is at best useful to summarily refer to a highly complex subject area. More specific empirical concepts are needed to enable us to acquire a thorough understanding of this area.

NOTES

1. On the history of the term in the USA cf. CLAUSEN (1968b: 21 ff.); WENTWORTH (1980); GEULEN (1991).

2. Cf. LACEY (1985).

3. German: "Sozialisiertheit."

4. ACHINGER and FELDMANN (1971: 136).

5. SÜSSMUTH (1969: 417).

6. LÜSCHER (1977: 591).

7. MÜNDER (1985: 11).

8. Examples were taken from NEIDHARDT (1970, 1970a and 1971); BRIM (1966); BERGER and LUCKMANN (1987); FEND (1971); RÖSSNER (1973 and 1977); ALLERBECK and ROSENMAYR (1976); IBEN (1975); KOB (1976); HURRELMANN (1977); GEULEN (1977); KNOLL (1978); HURRELMANN and ULICH (1980), etc.

9. CLAUSEN (1968a: 9); GILGENMANN (1986).

10. LIPPITT (1968: 349).

11. GEULEN (1973: 85).

12. Ordinance of the Ministry of Education on the Academic Examination for Teaching Positions in Gymnasia of 2 December 1977. *Gesetzblatt für Baden-Württemberg* No. 1/1978, p. 41.

13. BUBOLZ (1986: 151 ff.).

14. BUNDESMINISTER FÜR JUGEND, FAMILIE UND GESUNDHEIT (1975: 13). (Italics in original).

15. For our purposes we can ignore the fact that the term "socialization" is also applied to animals, plants and insects, cf., e.g., POIRIER (1972); CHEVALIER-SKOLNIKOFF and POIRIER (1977), especially BEKOFF (1977).

16. GEORGES (1962: 2701 f.); R. KLOTZ (1963, Vol. 2: 1365 f.).

17. GECK (1963: 23 f.). *Barnhart Dictionary of Etymology* (1988: 1029).

18. *Oxford English Dictionary*, 2nd ed. (1989, Vol. 15: 905 ff.).

19. ANDERSON (1964: 643). The term "socialization" appears as early as 1841. *Oxford English Dictionary*, 2nd ed. (1989, Vol. 15: 905 ff., 910).

20. GECK (1963). Naturally besides this loan word

German has its own word for social: "gesellig." "Society" is "Gesellschaft," and compound words are constructed using "gesellschafts" as a prefix. "To socialize," in the sense of nationalization, is "vergesellschaften."

21. Cf. SACHER (1931), ZIMMERMANN (1948), BÜLOW (1955), GECK (1963), KNOSPE (1972) as well as the most recent German lexica, such as *Brockhaus, Duden, Herder* and *Meyer*. The English usage is similar. Cf. leading English-language dictionaries, e.g., *Oxford English Dictionary, Longman, Chambers, Merriam-Webster, Barnhart, Funk and Wagnals, American Heritage, Random House,* etc.

22. *Oxford English Dictionary,* 2nd ed. (1989, Vol. 15: 905 ff.)

23. Cf. ZIMMERMANN (1948: 191); GECK (1963: 5 and 44 ff.); KNOSPE (1972: 709).

24. On these three aspects of the meanings of words cf. KAINZ (1962: 98).

25. RITTIG (1956: 455).

26. RITTIG (1956); NELL-BREUNING (1962).

27. *American Heritage Dictionary,* 2nd ed. (1982: 1160). *Oxford English Dictionary,* 2nd ed. (1989, Vol. 15: 910): "The action or fact of socializing or establishing upon a socialistic basis."

28. RITTIG (1956: 456 as well as 459 ff.); cf. also *Oxford English Dictionary,* 2nd ed. (1989, Vol. 15: 911): "to render socialistic in nature; to establish or develop according to the theories or principles of socialism." Cf. BESTOR (1948: 277 f.); SCHIEDER (1984); H. MÜLLER (1967); GECK (1963); CLAEYS (1986).

29. NELL-BREUNING (1962: col. 296).

30. KARRENBERG (1965: col. 1137).

31. SIMMEL (1910, 1971, 1983). This is the title of an article which appeared in English in the *American Journal of Sociology* (1910), translated by ALBION W. SMALL. Cf. also GIDDINGS (1897).

32. SIMMEL (1983: 23) (my italics). English: (1909 and 1971a). Cf. FRISBY (1992: 12 ff.) on "society as sociation (Vergesellschaftung)." Cf. SIMMEL (1950 and 1958).

33. Cf. OPPENHEIMER (1922/23: 425, 512 and 88).

FRANZ OPPENHEIMER (1864-1943) was a leading German sociologist.

34. LOCHNER (1975: 83 and 212). RUDOLF LOCHNER (1895-1978) was a German pedagogue who attempted to develop empirical theories of education.

35. MAX WEBER (1978: 26 and 1972: 13 ff., 21 ff.).

36. The comment, "Every new generation is like an attack by little barbarians" stems from FREDERIC LE PLAY (1806-82) and has been cited by many authors. Cf. OPPENHEIMER (1922: 88); WEISS (1929: 21); PARSONS (1951: 208) (without referring to LE PLAY); LOCHNER (1976: 136).

37. KANT (1963: 9).

38. WILLMANN (1980, Vol. 4: 70 and 1930). OTTO WILLMANN (1839-1920) was an important pedagogue at the German University of Prague who built on the ideas of both HERBART and SCHLEIERMACHER in trying to develop an empirical science of education. Cf. BREZINKA (1992: 37 and 209).

39. KANT (1963: 16 f. and 34).

40. McDOUGALL (1963: 16): "the moralisation of the individual by the society into which he is born as a creature in which the non-moral and purely egoistic tendencies are so much stronger than any altruistic tendencies."

41. GEULEN (1977).

42. Cf. ALLPORT (1955).

43. For a critique of inexact usage of this term cf. BUSEMANN (1935 and 1956); on more recent psychological terminological usage and its problematic cf. D. ULICH (1986).

44. German: "soziale Entwicklung."

45. GEULEN and HURRELMANN (1980: 58).

46. GEULEN (1980: 16).

47. HURRELMANN and ULICH (1980: 7 and 9) (my italics).

48. KOB (1976: 10 and 12).

49. BRIM (1966: 3) (my italics).

50. FRÖHLICH and WELLEK (1972: 681).

51. NEIDHARDT (1970: col. 1053).

52. PARSONS (1951: 201 ff.).

53. NIMKOFF (1964: 672).
54. BRIM (1966: 4 f.).
55. CLAESSENS (1967: 34).
56. MOLLENHAUER (1971: col. 1068).
57. FEND (1971: 114).
58. BUNDESMINISTER FÜR JUGEND (1975: 13).
59. ORBAN (1973: 6): "the manner in which the person acquires humanness, . . . which above all means socialization."
60. WURZBACHER (1963: 23, 14 and 27).
61. NEIDHARDT (1971: 6).
62. NEIDHARDT (1971: 5).
63. K. ULICH (1981: 344).
64. ALLERBECK and ROSENMAYR (1976: 81).
65. BERGER and LUCKMANN (1987: 150).
66. BRIM (1966: 5).
67. CHILD (1954: 655 and 682 ff.); GOSLIN (1969: 2).
68. WURZBACHER (1963: 12).
69. DOLLARD (1939: 69).
70. CLAUSEN (1968a: 6).
71. FEND (1969: 65 ff.).
72. HASSENSTEIN (1973: 80).
73. STIEGLITZ (1975).
74. Cf. BREZINKA (1994: 27 ff.); LONG and HADDEN (1985).
75. J. DEWEY (1968: 10 ff.).
76. Cf. KRIECK (1922: 13 and 1934: 11 ff.); F. SCHNEIDER (1953: 11 ff.). For a critique cf. BREZINKA (1994: 61 ff.).
77. PETERSEN (1924: 104); a similar view in WEISS (1929: 47 ff.).
78. DURKHEIM (1956: 71 f.).
79. RÖHRS (1973: 160 f. and 260).
80. Cf., e.g., the 28 June 1950 Constitution of Nordrhein-Westfalen Art. 8; 23 March 1976 School Law for Baden-Württemberg, § 1.
81. H. ROTH (1971: 590); HURRELMANN (1975: 11).
82. U. HERRMANN (1987: 55).
83. A. FLITNER (1977: 41).
84. NUNNER-WINKLER and ROLFF (1971: 177).

85. HEHLMANN (1971: 514).

86. K. ULICH (1981: 344).

87. KOB (1976: 9); similar MACHWIRTH (1974: 264); HURRELMANN (1975: 20).

88. STRZELEWICZ (1974: 182 and 188).

89. MÜHLBAUER (1986: 180).

90. HEHLMANN (1971: 514).

91. PRIEBE (1977: 177).

92. ROESSLER (1976: 17). Tending in this direction is GRUHL's 1983 dissertation: "Sozialisation als kategoriale Erfassung von Welt" [Socialization as Grasping the World in Categories].

93. BITTNER (1974: 325 f.).

94. Cf., e.g., SPIECKER (1976); RHONHEIMER (1977).

95. RHONHEIMER (1977: 43).

96. GIESECKE (1985: 12).

97. BITTNER (1974a: 391).

98. BACH (1975: 42).

99. GUKENBIEHL (1973: 76).

100. GEULEN (1973: 95 and 99).

101. NUNNER-WINKLER and ROLFF (1971: 198).

102. STIEGLITZ (1976).

103. RHONHEIMER (1977); cf. also SPIECKER (1976).

104. PARSONS (1951: 207 f.).

105. PARSONS (1951: 201, 205 and 207 ff.).

106. PARSONS and BALES (1964: 17).

107. Cf., e.g., PARSONS (1951: 154 and 209 ff.).

108. PARSONS (1951: 212).

109. PARSONS (1964: 130).

110. PARSONS (1964: 130). For a critique of the metaphor "role" cf. WILSHIRE (1977).

111. CHILD (1954: 655) (my italics).

112. Cf. BREZINKA (1994: 56).

113. Cf. CHILD (1954: 655 and 682 ff.).

114. CHILD (1954: 682 f.).

115. CHILD (1954: 681).

116. CHILD (1954: 655).

117. CHILD (1972: 762 f.) (my italics).

118. ZIGLER and CHILD (1969: 474) (my italics).

119. ELKIN (1960: 4) and ELKIN and HANDEL (1984: 4)

(my emphasis).

120. ELKIN (1960: 5) and ELKIN and HANDEL (1984: 8).

121. Cf. BUSEMANN (1935 and 1956); THOMAE (1959); MÜHLE (1969 and 1972).

122. ALLPORT (1937: 147).

123. Cf. BREZINKA (1994: 81 and 190 ff.).

124. BRIM (1966: 3) (my italics).

125. BRIM (1966: 4 f.).

126. BRIM (1966: 5).

127. BRIM (1966: 4).

128. BRIM (1966: 18).

129. BRIM (1966: 28, 25, 20).

130. BRIM (1966: 29 ff.).

131. BRIM (1966: 26 ff.).

132. BRIM (1966: 31 and 35).

133. CLAUSEN (1968a: 3 and 7).

134. CLAUSEN (1968a: 6) (my italics).

135. CLAUSEN (1968a: 7).

136. For a critique of the concept "self-education" cf. BREZINKA (1994: 75).

137. CLAUSEN (1968a: 7).

138. CLAUSEN (1968a: 3).

139. KRIECK (1922: 47).

140. GOSLIN (1971: 300).

141. GOSLIN (1969: 2).

142. GOSLIN (1971: 300) (my italics).

143. GOSLIN (1969: 4).

144. GOSLIN (1969: 5 and 1971: 302) (my italics).

145. INKELES (1969: 617).

146. INKELES (1969: 615) (my italics).

147. INKELES (1968: 82).

148. INKELES (1968: 93 ff.).

149. INKELES (1966: 280).

150. INKELES (1966: 279).

151. SECORD and BACKMAN (1974: 459 and 462).

152. SECORD and BACKMAN (1974: 462).

153. SECORD and BACKMAN (1974: 462 ff.), p. 463: "How social learning takes place is only partly understood."

154. SECORD and BACKMAN (1974: 461).

155. SECORD and BACKMAN (1974: 564).

156. WURZBACHER (1963: 12).
157. WURZBACHER (1963: 14). German: "soziale Prägung."
158. WURZBACHER (1963: 27): "Vorgang der vergesellschaftenden Prägung des Menschen durch die Gruppe."
159. WURZBACHER (1963: 23).
160. WURZBACHER (1963: 14).
161. WURZBACHER (1963: 12).
162. WURZBACHER (1963: 25 f.).
163. *American Heritage Dictionary*, 2nd ed. (1982: 581).
164. *American Heritage Dictionary*, 2nd ed. (1982: 240 and 1239).
165. *American Heritage Dictionary*, 2nd ed. (1982: 647). German: "prägen," meaning to stamp, imprint, form, determine.
166. CLAESSENS (1967: 34).
167. CLAESSENS (1967: 44).
168. CLAESSENS (1967: 134).
169. CLAESSENS (1967: 35).
170. CLAESSENS (1967: 14).
171. CLAESSENS (1967: 130).
172. CLAESSENS (1967: 38).
173. NEIDHARDT (1971: 5).
174. NEIDHARDT (1970a: 24).
175. *American Heritage Dictionary*, 2nd ed. (1982: 1286 and 1288).
176. NEIDHARDT (1970: 1053 f.) (my italics).
177. NEIDHARDT (1971: 6).
178. NEIDHARDT (1970a: 23).
179. NEIDHARDT (1970a: 23 and 1971: 5 ff.).
180. HABERMAS (1973: 118).
181. HABERMAS (1973: 120, 132, 122).
182. HABERMAS (1973: 140 ff.).
183. MOLLENHAUER (1971: 1068 f.).
184. MOLLENHAUER (1969: 271).
185. MOLLENHAUER (1969: 286 and 271 ff.).
186. MOLLENHAUER (1971: col. 1071) (my italics).
187. MOLLENHAUER (1969: 271, 286, 288, 293, 281).
188. FEND (1969: 33 ff.).

189. FEND (1969: 38).

190. FEND (1969: 44).

191. FEND (1969: 55); similar is also FEND (1971a: 17).

192. FEND (1971: 113).

193. FEND (1971: 114).

194. FEND (1974: 12).

195. FEND (1974: 15).

196. FEND (1974: 13).

197. FEND (1974: 13).

198. FEND (1974: 20).

199. FEND (1974: 29).

200. FEND (1974: 15).

201. FEND (1974: 29).

202. FEND (1974 : 38) (my italics).

203. FEND (1974: 36 and 38).

204. FEND (1974: 31).

205. FEND (1974: 15).

206. FEND (1974: 41). "Complementary" actually means "supplementary," which makes no sense here. Presumably intended is the sense of interrelated, appearing together or in a mutually conditioned manner.

207. FEND (1974: 16).

208. BREZINKA (1994: 55 ff.).

209. H. ROTH (1971: 365).

210. H. ROTH (1971: 479).

211. H. ROTH (1971: 480).

212. H. ROTH (1967: 197).

213. H. ROTH (1971: 480).

214. H. ROTH (1971: 590).

215. H. ROTH (1969: 22).

216. H. ROTH (1971: 590).

217. KUCKARTZ (1969: 9).

218. Cf., e.g., KUCKARTZ (1969: 9, 56, 145).

219. KUCKARTZ (1969: 181, 188, 143).

220. Presumably KUCKARTZ borrowed the expression from GEHLEN (1988: 51), where it is asserted that man's inner life is under "pressure to form" ("Formierungszwang").

221. GEORGES (1962: col. 2819).

222. American Heritage Dictionary, 2nd ed. (1982: 525

f.), also"to come to have; develop: *form a habit.*"

223. *American Heritage Dictionary,* 2nd ed. (1982: 526).

224. KUCKARTZ (1969: 137 and 182).

225. KUCKARTZ (1969: 171).

226. KUCKARTZ (1969: 188).

227. KUCKARTZ (1969: 189 f.).

228. KUCKARTZ (1969: 190).

229. KUCKARTZ (1969: 187): "Education is . . . rationalized socialization."

230. For a critique cf. BREZINKA (1994: 55 ff.).

231. KUCKARTZ (1969: 177).

232. KUCKARTZ (1969: 187).

233. DURKHEIM (1972: 30 and 1973: 46).

234. KUCKARTZ (1969: 189).

235. KUCKARTZ (1969: 185).

236. KUCKARTZ (1969: 189).

237. FRÖHLICH and WELLEK (1972: 661).

238. FRÖHLICH and WELLEK (1972: 663).

239. FRÖHLICH and WELLEK (1972: 664).

240. FRÖHLICH and WELLEK (1972: 662, 673, 671).

241. FRÖHLICH and WELLEK (1972: 680).

242. FRÖHLICH and WELLEK (1972: 672) (my italics).

243. FRÖHLICH and WELLEK (1972: 681).

244. RÖSSNER (1977: 103).

245. RÖSSNER (1977: 104 f.) (my italics).

246. RÖSSNER (1977: 105).

247. RÖSSNER (1977: 105).

248. Cf., e.g., RÖSSNER (1977: 172, footnote 199).

249. Cf. BREZINKA (1994: 141 ff.); likewise RÖSSNER (1977: 28 ff.).

250. RÖSSNER (1977: 107).

251. Cf. BREZINKA (1994: 86).

252. RÖSSNER (1977: 104 ff. and 129).

253. Cf., e.g., RÖSSNER (1973: 147 and 246).

254. RÖSSNER (1973: 145).

255. GEULEN (1973: 87). "Persönlichkeitsgenese."

256. GEULEN (1973: 86 f.).

257. GEULEN (1973: 93).

258. GEULEN (1973: 95 ff.).

259. GEULEN (1973: 99).

260. KOB (1976: 9 and 7) (my italics).

261. KOB (1976: 10 f.).

262. KOB (1976: 9 f.).

263. KOB (1976: 12) (my italics).

264. KOB (1976: 11).

265. KOB (1976: 11).

266. KOB (1976: 9 and 11).

267. Cf. BREZINKA (1994: 55 ff.).

268. KOB (1976: 19).

269. KOB (1976: 49).

270. KOB (1976: 81).

271. KOB (1976: 58).

272. KOB (1976: 67).

273. KOB (1976: 61).

274. KOB (1976: 49).

275. *American Heritage Dictionary*, 2nd ed. (1982: 651).

276. KOB (1976: 41). The text states, due to a typographical error: "intended side effect." From the context (cf. also p. 49) it is, however, clear that an "unintended" side effect is meant.

277. KOB (1976: 19) (my italics).

278. *American Heritage Dictionary*, 2nd ed. (1982: 924).

279. KOB (1976: 25).

280. KOB (1976: 24).

281. Cf., e.g., HESS (1975: esp. 417 ff.); LOCHNER (1975: 63 ff.).

282. Cf. R. KÖNIG (1974: 102 and 109); (1955: 127 and 145).

283. Cf., e.g., the subtitle of CLAESSENS (1967) and in the same volume on page 13: "The concept of the 'second, socio-cultural birth' of the person."

284. On linguistic seduction by metaphors cf. KAINZ (1972: 99 ff.).

285. R. KÖNIG (1955: 145 ff.); (1974: 101 f. and 109).

286. Cf., e.g., MÄRZ (1978: 97, 142, 211). The image of the "second birth of children, the spiritual" goes back to HEGEL (1830: 320, § 521).

287. HEINZ (1976: 412).
288. HEINZ (1976: 416).
289. HEINZ (1976: 415).
290. KNOLL (1978: 728).
291. KNOLL (1978: 735).
292. KNOLL (1978: 728).
293. HURRELMANN (1975: 11).
294. HURRELMANN (1975: 14).
295. HURRELMANN (1975: 20).
296. Cf., e.g., HURRELMANN (1975: 76).
297. HURRELMANN (1975: 20).
298. For a semantic analysis of the word "aim" cf. BREZINKA (1994: 110 ff.).
299. HURRELMANN (1975: 14).
300. Cf. in this book p. 4 f.
301. D. ULICH (1976: 64).
302. OEVERMANN (1979: 145).
303. On the process of conceptual explication cf. BREZINKA (1994: 22 ff.).
304. *American Heritage Dictionary*, 2nd ed. (1982: 987).
305. BALDWIN (1960, Vol. 2: 356).
306. EISLER (1929, Vol. 2: 505).
307. KLAUS and BUHR (1975: 990).
308. *American Heritage Dictionary*, 2nd ed. (1982: 860).
309. Cf. ROHRACHER (1963: 7): "Every mental phenomenon is either a process or a state."
310. *American Heritage Dictionary*, 2nd ed. (1982: 987).
311. *American Heritage Dictionary*, 2nd ed. (1982: 1190).
312. Cf. THOMAE (1959); MÜHLE (1969: 82 ff.).
313. BUSEMANN (1935: 49 and 1956: 27 ff.); cf. also DREVER and FRÖHLICH (1977: 105 f.).
314. Cf. ALLPORT (1955).
315. GEULEN (1973: 93).
316. BRIM (1966: 3).
317. HABERMAS (1973: 118 ff.).
318. Cf. GEULEN and HURRELMANN (1980: 58 and 51 f.).

319. INKELES (1969: 615).

320. Cf. BREZINKA (1994: 56 ff.).

321. For a clarification cf. BREZINKA (1994: 66 ff.).

322. This vague concept is broader than the concept of education and includes care. To be sure some authors understand by "child rearing" not actions, but rather "interactions between parents and children . . . which— intended or not—prepare the child for its future life": SEARS/MACCOBY/LEVIN (1977: 13 and 1957). In this case it is especially false to use the expression "child rearing" interchangeably with "education."

323. German: "Gebildetsein" or "Gebildetheit." Cf. BREZINKA (1988: 30). Here the word "Bildung" is being discussed, which refers to culture, refinement, higher levels of education, in general to the ideal state of being educated, rather than the process of education.

324. LOCHNER (1975: 211).

325. LOCHNER (1975: 213).

326. BERGER and LUCKMANN (1987: 157, 183): "Totally successful socialization is anthropologically impossible."

327. Cf. BREZINKA (1994: 93).

328. Cf. RYLE (1952: 149 ff.).

329. Cf. BREZINKA (1981: 106 ff.).

330. WURZBACHER (1963); NEIDHARDT (1970: col. 1054).

331. WURZBACHER (1963).

332. McDOUGALL (1908: 16).

333. PÖGGELER (1964: 22): "becoming an adult."

334. A similar term, "lingualize," exists in phonetics but with a different sense. *Oxford English Dictionary*, 2nd ed. (1989, Vol. 8: 991).

335. The word "professionalize" currently means "to render or make professional." *Oxford English Dictionary*, 2nd ed. (1989, Vol. 12: 574).

336. A similar term already exists, "religionize." *Oxford English Dictionary*, 2nd ed. (1989, Vol. 13: 570).

337. The word "musicalization" already exists in the sense of "the expression or rendering of an art (other than music) in the style or manner of music." *Oxford English Dictionary*, 2nd ed. (1989, Vol. 10: 129).

338. Similar to the existing term "sexualize" meaning

"to make sexual, endow with sex, attribute sex to." *Oxford English Dictionary*, 2nd ed. (1989, Vol. 15: 116).

339. Also called "gender-role socialization."

340. *American Heritage Dictionary*, 2nd ed. (1982: 1160).

341. For a critique of the confusion of results (or the end of a process) with aims cf. RICKERT (1922: 121).

342. Basic to this N. HARTMANN (1966: 19 ff. and 64 ff.).

343. N. HARTMANN (1966: 27).

344. Cf. MONTADA (1982: 48 ff.).

345. Cf. D. ULICH (1986: 25).

346. This also applies in essence to the words "enculturation," "moralization," etc. Cf., e.g., *Oxford English Dictionary*, 2nd ed. (1989, Vol. 9: 1071): Moralization is "the action of making moral or more moral; the process of becoming moral."

347. Cf. BREZINKA (1981: 115 ff.).

348. Cf. on this the critique by D. ULICH (1976: 65).

349. Similar view in FRÖHLICH and WELLEK (1972: 681).

350. Thus also GEULEN and HURRELMANN (1980: 55 ff.).

.

2

"Models" in Educational Theories: A Contribution to the Clarification of Concepts

In the last few years the word "model" has been employed with increasing frequency in pedagogical texts. We read for example of "educational models," "educational planning models" and "model construction"; of "model instruction" and "instructional models," "didactic models," "scheduling models," "models of curriculum development" and "model curricula"; of "model conceptions," "model plans," "model awareness" and "model interpretations"; of "thought models" and "models of thinking"; of "Modell-Lernen" (imitative learning), "models of teaching" and "learning models"; of "model behavior" and "behavior models"; of "model schools" and "school models"; of "model experiments," "model projects," "model conditions," "model development," "model construction," "model building," "model planning," "model programs," "model methods," "model testing," "model implementation," "model evaluation" and "model accompanying research."

We come across books with titles like *Analyses and Models for School Reform* (Analysen und Modelle zur Schulreform, Hentig 1966), *Models of Modern Educational Policy* (Modelle moderner Bildungspolitik, Evers 1969), *Theories and Models of Didactics* (Theorien und Modelle der Didaktik, Blankertz 1975), *Models of Emancipatory Education* (Modelle emanzipatorischer Erziehung, Kerstiens 1974), *Models of Instructional Methods* (Modelle der Unterrichtsmethode, H. Geissler 1977), *Models of Pedagogical Understanding* (Modelle pädagogischen Verstehens, Loch 1978), *Models of Pedagogical Theory Construction* (Modelle pädagogischer Theorienbildung, Blass 1978), *Models of Thinking and Learning* (Modelle des Denkens und Lernens, Spada 1976), *Thinking in Models* (In Modellen denken, Halbfas 1976), *Thinking in Models* (Denken in Modellen, Schaefer/Trommer/Wenk 1977), *Psychological Modelling* (Bandura 1971), *Models and Model Thinking in Instruction* (Modelle und Modelldenken im Unterricht, Stachowiak 1980), *Model and Methods in Empirical Educational Research* (Modell und Methode in der empirischen Erziehungsforschung, Lehmann 1977).

In addition, there are many further combinations like "model types" and "type models"; "model person," "model case," "model level," "model allegiance," "model variant," "model optimization," "model correction" and "model inventory"; "guiding model," "cooperation model," "preparatory model," "planning model," "explication model," "functional model," "organizational model," "basic model," "element model," "elementary model," "core model," "type model," "universal model," "innovation model," "structural model," "descriptive model," "analytic model," "conceptual model," "action model," "interaction model," "representation model," "verification model," "analogy model," "categorial model," "science model," "feedback model," "mental model," "teacher models" and "pupil models." We read of "model constructors" or "model builders" and "model users," etc. All the cited expressions stem from the *pedagogical* texts on which this analysis is based.

Although recently the word "model" has been extensively employed in pedagogics, just as it has in many other sciences, what it means in a given text can seldom be recognized with any immediacy or certainty. There is no generally known and accepted rule for its employment. Already in everyday language and especially in scientific terminology it has very diverse meanings. Therefore whenever we come across the word "model" in a text we should attempt to determine what it means for the respective author. This would be easy if everyone who used the word "model" in pedagogical texts or discourse would state what they personally intend it to mean. Unfortunately this is only rarely the case. We encounter not only various meanings, but also a reluctance to explain one's own model concept. In some cases this reluctance probably arises because users of the word "model" are insufficiently clear about its meaning and have at best rather vague notions of how to use it.

Lack of clarity in the use of the term "model" impedes communication and causes unnecessary difficulties in the study of pedagogical texts. In order to alleviate these problems, conceptual clarification is needed. The first step in this direction is to recognize the present lack of clarity and examine its extent. To begin with, we must collect and classify the meanings associated with the word "model" in pedagogical usage. This will help us to obtain an overview of the model concepts found in educational theories and to evaluate these concepts from the viewpoint of logical precision.

As a second step, the different model concepts must be evaluated from the practical viewpoint of their particular usefulness. This is a matter of determining whether a given concept is fruitful. Also to be decided is whether its conceptual contents are appropriately designated by the word "model." Associating a concept with this term is unnecessary if another expression or term is already in use for the concept which is better understood than "model."[1]

Since the word "model" has been borrowed by the authors of pedagogical texts partly from everyday language and partly from the terminology of other sciences, we must begin with a look at extra-pedagogical usage.

MEANINGS OF THE WORD "MODEL" OUTSIDE OF PEDAGOGICS

On Etymology and Extra-Scientific Usage

Etymologically the word "model" has its origin in the Latin word "modus,"[2] which meant a "unit adopted as a standard of measurement." It derives from Indo-Euro-

pean "met-," which also produced "measure" and "metre."
The meanings broadened to include "size," "limit," "way,"
"method," "unit of time as the basis of a rhythm, measure; (esp. in poetry or elaborate prose)," a speech rhythm, a musical interval, a "sequence of intervals forming
a scale or tune," a "pipe of specified diameter used to
control the rate of flow of water," a standard, plan, rule,
requirement, example, pattern, form. In Medieval Latin it
meant a custom, manner, mould or model.[3] A variant
was "modellus." From the Latin came Old French "modelle," Middle French "modèle," and Italian "modello," which
were borrowed by English. In English "model" first meant
"architects' plans." In the early seventeenth century it acquired the sense of "three-dimensional representation,"
and "artist's model" developed in the latter part of that
century. A variant of Latin "modulus" is Old French
"modle" with the variant "molle" from which French
"moule" is derived and from which we have Middle English "molde," whence English "mould."[4] "Model" can
mean a "representation of structure," a "type of design,"
an "object of imitation," etc. Other words deriving from
"modus" are "modern," "modicum," "modify" and "mode."[5]

In *architecture* the word "model" refers to "an archi-
tect's set of designs (plans, elevations, sections, etc.) for
a projected building," a "representation in three dimensions of some projected or existing structure . . . showing
the proportions and arrangement of its component
parts."[6] Two dimensional drawings, e.g., blueprints, are
usually not called "models."

For artistic activities such as *painting* and *sculpture* a
"model" is an object of nature or culture, especially a
person who poses for an artistic representation or work
of art. In sculpture, however, a small preliminary version
of a plastic is also referred to as a "model" for the larger
final version; likewise also a pattern in the final size
which is poured in plaster and transferred to wood or
stone or cast in bronze.

For *craftsmen* a "model" is a pattern according to
which a specific class of objects is manufactured. Examples of this are hollow forms such as casting, printing or

baking forms and also paper patterns for weaving, embroidery, lace making or sewing. In handicraft model building is a skilled trade; in German industry one can be employed as a *Modelltischler* (cabinetmaker who constructs wooden models) or *Modellschlosser* (a craftsman who constructs models out of metal). Such professional craftsmen prepare models of wood, metal, plaster, clay, rubber or plastic for metal casting and also build experimental, teaching and display models.

In *manufacturing technology* "models" are understood, on the one hand, as visible (material) designs or patterns for the (mass) production of products and, on the other hand, as representations or copies of products in reduced, natural or enlarged dimensions. A "working model" is "one so constructed as to imitate the movements of the machine which it represents."[7] Working models can serve as experimental objects (e.g., an airplane model which is observed in a wind tunnel), as instructional means (e.g., cross-sectional models of machines) or as toys (e.g., scale model trains, autos, ships, etc.). Likewise, the first example of a planned product (e.g., a machine or motor vehicle) is called a "model" in the sense of "prototype": it is "a preliminary pattern serving as the plan from which an item not yet constructed will be produced."[8] In addition, "a particular type of vehicle, weapon, machine, instrument, etc., as made by a particular maker" is a model. Thus automobile manufacturers produce cars in various "models," and regularly introduce "new models."[9]

In elevated *everyday language* (cultured usage) the word "model" also has the sense of a (good) example, exemplar, ideal or norm, "a person, or a work, that is proposed or adopted for imitation,"[10] e.g., a "model student." In this sense, a "model" is something that (through its degree of perfection, exemplariness, etc.) can serve as a pattern or example for something or someone else. Thus one can say that a country is or has become a model of liberal democracy (or for a liberal democracy), that it can serve as a model for other countries. Model institutions or organizations can be used as a basis for setting up, structuring, organizing or reforming other institutions or organizations.[11]

These examples suffice to show that already in extra-scientific usage the word "model" has very diverse meanings. The central attribute of a model in the language of craft and technique is that it is a three-dimensional *copy* of an object. This model concept refers to "an accurate scale, similar, in general reduced copy" of a specific given object, a "material system," an original.[12] On the other hand, however, in artistic contexts *originals* are also referred to as "models" (e.g., persons or things that are portrayed by artists). Likewise in normative everyday language it is not the imperfect copy, but rather the (usually only imagined) *original image* (*Urbild*) or *ideal* which is regarded as a "model."

Common to these various model concepts is only that a model is in every case an object which has a relationship of *similarity* (or of analogy) to another object. A model is always a model *of* or *for* something.

On Usage in the Empirical Sciences

In the natural sciences the term "model" has been used with increasing frequency since the nineteenth century and has in the meantime acquired many new senses.[13] These senses range from "model as a means of visualizing a theory" to "model as a means of setting up, further developing and applying a theory"[14] to "model as theory." Thus in the words of the *Oxford English Dictionary*, a model is "a simplified or idealized description or conception of a particular system, situation, or process (often in mathematical terms: so *mathematical model*) that is put forward as a basis for calculations, predictions, or further investigation."[15] In the twentieth century one also speaks increasingly of "models" in the social and cultural sciences, especially in economics, psychology, sociology and political science, as well as in linguistics.[16] Since the middle of the twentieth century such vast numbers of philosophy of science (or meta-scientific) texts have been published on model concepts and the theory of models, that even specialists can scarcely get an overview of the topic.[17] The term "model" has for some time ceased to be primarily a serious term, having become one of the most widely used scientific fashion words. "Model building is science 'à la mode'."[18] With some delay this fashion has also reached the science of education.

It would be impossible to list here all the senses in which the word "model" is employed by the various empirical sciences and disciplines. Already in 1962 a linguist could list thirty-nine different senses.[19] While some agree at least to a certain extent, others are mutually exclusive. In this situation every attempt to achieve clarity must begin with the insight that today there is less reason than ever before to postulate a *single*, universal model concept. There is no single dominant concept, not even within the context of a particular empirical science. To the contrary, the word "model" is used as a term for a multitude of different concepts. Not only do these concepts have various contents, they are also employed for various purposes (or have various functions).[20]

Nevertheless, some scholars have actually tried to devise "universal model concepts."[21] After first collecting as many senses of the word "model" as they can, they attempt to determine a set of common conceptual attributes. Given the existing wealth of meanings, it must be expected from the start that such efforts to grasp the "conceptual essence of the word 'model'"[22] can at best produce only extremely content-poor model concepts. Accordingly, "universal model concepts" are defined using so few attributes that they are applicable to far too many different objects, but say almost nothing specific about them.

As an example we can use the "universal model concept" which Stachowiak arrived at on the basis of a semantic analysis of the word "model."[23] He defined his model concept in terms of the following three chief attributes:

1. "Representational attribute": "Models are always models *of something*, namely depictions or representations of natural or artificial originals which again can themselves

be models." The originals "can belong to the domain of symbols, the world of conceptions and concepts or to physical reality."

2. "Abbreviation attribute": "Models generally do *not* comprehend *all* the attributes of the original they represent, but rather only those which appear relevant to the respective model creators and/or model users." Other authors speak more aptly of "simplification."

3. "Pragmatic attribute": "Models are not per se uniquely related to their originals. They serve as a substitute for their object (a) for *specific* knowing and/or acting model-using *subjects*, (b) within *specific time intervals* and (c) limited to *specific mental or physical activities*." Models are therefore not only models of something, but also "models *for someone*." They are further "models *for a specific purpose*." Simply stated: a model is created by a subject for a purpose.

This "universal model concept" is therefore so comprehensively stated that it can be applied to a great variety of concrete and abstract objects. These range from two-dimensional "graphic models," for example, pictures and diagrams, to three-dimensional "technical models," from globes on up to animal experiments, and may even include abstract "semantic models." Among the "semantic models" falling under the concept are not only linguistic models, but also "perceptual models" and "cogitative models," thus peoples' perceptually and intellectually influenced and determined conceptual complexes. However, by no means all types of models are covered by Stachowiak's "universal model concept." Rather, through the "representational attribute," the concept of model is limited to depictions, thereby excluding from its area of application original images, designs and pattern forms. Furthermore, the "pragmatic attribute" precludes all logico-semantic senses of the word "model" in which no subjects or purposes are given, but only a logically postulated relationship between model and object.

Despite the seeming inconsistency of excluding such

senses from a "universal concept," Stachowiak believes in the almost unlimited "breadth and wealth" of his "universal model concept": "the most elementary perceptual givens" are "models" just as much "as the most complicated, comprehensive theory." He is of the view "that all cognition is *cognition in models* and/or *through models*, that every human contact with the world occurs through the medium of the model."[24] Probably only someone who advocates "modelism"[25] as a "cognitive concept" and world view would be interested in a model concept so vague that it could refer to almost any phenomena.

In contrast to Stachowiak, after having similarly attempted a harmonization at the highest level of generality of the meanings of the various model concepts employed in the empirical sciences, other authors openly admit that such a "universal model concept" is not very fruitful.[26] Fruitfulness is only to be expected from the adoption of more precisely defined, less general or more specific concepts.[27]

A concept is made more specific through the addition of definitional attributes. With an increase in the number of its attributes (intension), the extension of a concept narrows, i.e., there is a decrease in the range of things to which it can be applied. We can achieve an initial specification (or determination) of the term "model" by introducing the attribute "scientific," thereby precluding senses such as "model as pattern (or plan) for the manufacture of products." Furthermore, all senses of "model" must be excluded for which there already exist other, generally recognized terms. Therefore "the universal concept of the scientific model" must be so defined that its referents do not fall under concepts like "theory," "hypothesis," "mathematical description," "formal (or formalized) system," etc.[28]

As an example of a model concept more precisely defined in this sense I refer to Stoff's definition: "By a model is understood an ideally conceived or materially realized system which reflects or reproduces the research object, and is so suitable to stand for it, that its study gives us new information about this object."[29] Here the use of models as *means for acquiring knowledge* is an essential attribute which excludes other purposes. One should note that the last element of the definition narrows the concept quite unrealistically by specifying the attribute of success: if no new information is obtained from a model, Stoff's concept is inapplicable. Furthermore the definition does not satisfy the rule that the words used in defining a term (the "definiens") must be clearer than the term to be defined (the "definiendum"): Stoff's definition employs the words "system" and "reflect," which are no clearer than "model," the term they are intended to define.

Less ambiguous than the terms "reflect" and "stand for" (used by Stoff) or "representation" and "substitute" (used by Stachowiak) is the concept of *similarity* or *analogy*. The word "analogy" is understood with regard to models as the similarity in terms of certain attributes of objects which, apart from these attributes, differ in all respects.[30] Every object on which a model is based or for which a model is employed is called an original. The relationship between original and model is in each case an analogy with regard to the structure, function or behavior of the original.[31] Although models reproduce their objects in idealized form, "the characteristics, interactions and relations of the elements in a model must be analogous or similar to those in the object of study." The construction of models ("model construction," "constitution of models," "modelling") requires analogical insight. Without thinking by means of analogies, models cannot be created. In using analogies one should take into account that they reproduce the object of study only approximately, roughly and in a simplified manner. A model and its original are not identical, but only (more or less) similar.[32]

The attribute of analogy is, for example, employed in the following definition by Klaus and Buhr:[33] A model is "an object which is introduced by a subject on the basis of a structural, functional or behavioral analogy to a corresponding original and makes it possible to fulfill a specific task whose completion through direct operations on the original is at present impossible, may never be possible or under given conditions is too difficult."

Upon critical examination this model concept proves to be of much greater generality than the previously outlined concept of scientific model. This is due to the different statements made about the purposes of models. In the case of Stoff's concept of the scientific model, the original is a "research object," and the purpose of the model is to further the acquisition of "new information." In the case of the universal model concept proposed by Klaus and Buhr, the nature of the original is not precisely defined, and the purpose of a model is to aid in the accomplishment of a specific "task." The acquisition of new knowledge or "new information about the original" is in this case only one of several purposes (or one of several "functions of models"). Besides this, the authors name seven further purposes for employing models, among them demonstration (transmission of already known information to uninformed persons), the guidance of production, or the realization of a corresponding original, etc.[34]

This example shows again that universal model concepts are not only so poor in information as to be almost useless, but also misleading, if one supposes them capable of accounting for all possible ends which are pursued using the very different objects called "models." An object referred to as a "model" which very accurately depicts or copies the essential features of a real, existing original is essentially different from an object, likewise called a "model," which as a purely intellectual conception represents an original that does not yet exist and perhaps never will (as a mere conceived entity or product of the imagination). As an example, one thinks of "future models" of societies (utopias).[35] Only in the first case of "model as copy" is "similarity with an original" an essential attribute of the model concept.

An adequately precise model concept can only be created through choosing just *one* of several basic meanings of the word "model" and thereby sacrificing all other meanings. An example of this is the specification of the scientific concept of "model" with the assistance of the concept of *isomorphism* between theories.[36] The word "isomorphism," which is derived from Greek (*isos* meaning equal; *morphe* meaning shape), means "similarity in appearance or structure" (up to the special case of structural identity). The concept of isomorphism implies that a relatively well developed theory about a specific object can be a "model" for a theory about another, as yet less well-researched object, provided that, despite the difference in the nature of this object and its elements, there is a structural similarity between the nomological statements of both theories.[37] Thus one can, for example, employ a theory about how mice learn in mazes or Skinner boxes as a model for a theory of human learning. Explanations of how electronic computers calculate can provide models for theories of human thinking processes and their research. Conversely, theories of how the brain functions can be used to design more powerful "supercomputers."

A model thus means in this context not, as with Stachowiak, Stoff and Klaus and Buhr, a copy of an original, a "reflection" of reality, but rather an isomorphic theory about objects in a particular area, insofar as it is drawn on as a means of acquiring knowledge in a substantively different, but structurally similar area of study. The presupposition for the choice of a model in this sense is a hypothesis postulating structural similarities between the two areas. An example is the hypothesis that there is a structural similarity between schools and businesses. Based on this hypothesis, theories of business management have been used as models for the improvement of school theory.[38]

On Usage in the Formal Sciences of Logic and Mathematics

In the formal disciplines of logic and semantics, as well as in mathematics and theories of the foundations of mathematics (meta-mathematics), model concepts are employed which differ greatly from those used in the empirical sciences.[39] In these disciplines the term "model" refers essentially to non-verbal entities which realize a verbally given axiomatic-deductive statement system.

According to Tarski, "a possible realization in which all valid sentences of a theory T are satisfied is called a *model* of T."[40] One can only speak of a model in this sense if an axiomatically formulated theoretical system is present. In formal language this model concept can be expressed as follows: "By a model, or more precisely stated, a realization of an axiom system, will be understood a domain B in which the functions, relationships, etc. which are referred to in the axiom system are so interpreted that the axioms in B hold true."[41]

Some philosophers of science hold the view that logico-mathematical (or logico-semantic) model concepts should also be used in the empirical sciences,[42] to the exclusion of others. It can be objected, however, that such a privileging of these model concepts "in no way does justice to widespread scientific usage. This would exclude numerous structures of knowledge which, in the sense of representational theory, are certainly regarded as models, merely because a strict theory, whose accompanying model they would be, cannot as yet be explicitly stated." But, nevertheless, in many cases where such a theory is lacking, "empirical (and technical) model constructs specifically contribute to the formulation and development of theories."[43]

MEANINGS OF THE WORD "MODEL" IN PEDAGOGICS AND PHILOSOPHY OF EDUCATIONAL KNOWLEDGE

The term "pedagogics" (educology) refers to theories of education in the broad sense of the word "theory." These include practical, scientific and philosophical theories of education. Such theories can themselves be made the object of a theory, one called the meta-theory of education, meta-pedagogics (meta-educology), or philosophy of educational knowledge. The focus of this theory is the epistemological philosophy of pedagogical statement systems.[44]

As mentioned, the material in pedagogical texts where the word "model" is a significant term is already quite extensive. Therefore it cannot be comprehensively summarized here. I limit myself to presenting the results of an analysis and cite only a few texts as support.

In pedagogical and meta-pedagogical theories chiefly the following senses of the word "model" are currently employed.

"Model" as Means of Instruction, Teaching Aid

In theories of instruction a "model" is understood first of all as a means of visual representation. One can distinguish between "replica models" and "symbolic models."[45] A "replica model" looks "in some respect" like "the thing being modeled." For this reason it is also called an "iconic model" (from the Greek "eikonikos," meaning pictorial, viewable).[46] It is a visual material (or substantive) copy in simplified form of a given object of reality (an original). Thus, for example, a globe is a replica model of the earth.

In the narrowest sense of the term "model" a three-dimensional replica is meant.[47] It is known that models of this sort have a greater effect on the comprehension and retention of information than does pictorial illustration.[48] The possibilities for instructional presentation range over a continuum from the concrete presentation of an object itself to purely abstract representation. Instruction is decreasingly effective the less concrete and more abstract it becomes, as suggested by the following sequence: contact with the original (bringing it into the classroom or encountering it outside the school)—model—picture (statue, photograph or film)—language (oral presentation by a teacher).[49]

In a broader sense of the term two-dimensional replicas, drawings and sketches also count as "replica models." Where the original is unavailable, instruction must employ representational models. These serve not only as illustrations, but can also contribute to the structuring and simplification of the subject matter to be learned.[50]

This is even more the case with "symbolic models." Employing abstract symbols to represent either parts of objects or relationships among phenomena, symbolic models are visually different from their originals. We can use cartographic symbols as examples. A small circle drawn on a map looks different than the church whose location it indicates, an oblong rectangle different than a train station.

Symbolic models serve above all to clarify factual contents which are in themselves inaccessible to the senses. Unlike the abstract concepts for which they are introduced, they are physically present and thereby offer at least a minimum of concreteness.

For all instructional subjects there exist countless diagrams, schema, tables, illustrations, etc. as teaching materials. Thus symbolic models are also employed instructionally in the subjects of "pedagogics," "didactics," "educational psychology," etc. A familiar example is the so-called "didactic triangle," which symbolizes the relationships among teacher, pupil and subject matter.[51]

A model used as means of instruction is sometimes called a "didactic model."[52] This term is, however, ambiguous, as it can also refer to other things, e.g., *schemas* used to clarify didactic matters (ones related to instructional theory). At present, it is used chiefly in referring to *theories* of instruction.[53]

"Model" as an Object of Imitation

Educational theories have traditionally affirmed that children, to a large extent, *learn through imitation.* "The child, who still has no control of his reason, cannot do other than imitate what he sees and hears of other people."[54] The behavior which is (actually or possibly) imitated is usually called an "example." Through their social partners, everyone is also surrounded by examples for specific behaviors. These can be imitated either spontaneously and unconsciously or deliberately and intentionally. For their part, those persons whose behaviors serve as examples for imitation can set an example either unintentionally, without being aware of their influence, or, to the contrary, with the full intention of doing so. Examples and the consequences of following them can be judged on the basis of value standards. Since some examples have good and others bad effects on their imitators, it is the duty of educators to themselves set good examples, and beyond that, to also bring other good examples into the life circles of educands and to exclude bad examples. They can bring them into contact with real persons, show pictures of or give verbal reports on persons not physically present or even use fictious persons as examples.[55]

What until recently was called "learning from examples through imitation" or similarly designated[56] is currently called chiefly "imitative learning" (also "observational learning") from "models" and "learning from a model" (Modell-Lernen).[57] For the word "example" has been substituted "model behavior"; for the person imitated, the "model person," the "model for imitation" or the "learning model." This substitution of terms is itself a case of "imitative learning" from "models": by imitatively adopting the terminology of a branch of American psychology, namely that of social-learning theory. In this terminology parents are "living models" for their children, teachers "living models" for pupils,[58] or favorable or "unfavorable perceptual models for their pupils' learning."[59] Teachers are called on to "create realistic and symbolic models!"[60] But, it must be noted, educators cannot be other than "models," i.e., objects of possible (potential) imitation—regardless of whether they want to be or not.

Unlike many other senses of the word "model," in this case what is called a "model" is not a copy or imitation of an "original," but rather the "original" itself (or the "Urbild," i.e., the original image, instead of the "copy").

"Model" as Prototype

A prototype is an "original type, form, or instance . . . on which later stages are based or judged."[61] This sense is commonly employed in industrial technology (from the

Greek, meaning "original," "first form," "Urbild")[62]. It is used for the first operating models of products which, having been tested and under certain circumstances also improved, will eventually be produced in lots or even mass produced. "Model" is sometimes used in this sense pedagogically: "We also speak of model schools and model curricula in a comparable sense,"[63] i.e., in the sense of "prototype."

Texts on educational politics and school organization often refer to "model schools,"[64] "model kindergartens,"[65] the "model character" of educational institutions[66] and "model trials."[67]

Some authors conceive of "model schools" not as prototypes, but as schools which "experiment with special problems of didactics" or "with those of school organization."[68] They use the term "model school" as synonymous with "experimental school."[69]

Other authors, however, specifically use the term "model school" in referring to something other than an "experimental school," which has "the character of an experiment" or "an experimental character."[70] One author writes: "The model school displays, in contrast to the experimental school, what has been *tested*, an instructional method carefully tested for success and the corresponding school organization. It is there to serve as a *model* for all teachers."[71] It helps to create public awareness of the valuable results of *successful* experiments: "The setting up of experimental schools and school experiments is only sensible, if the results of successful experiments can be applied in 'model schools' or 'example schools,' which should make the tested results accessible to the broader pedagogical public."[72]

In the real world most experimental schools have more than just "trial character," for they are established with the well-grounded expectation that, if the experiment succeeds, they will become "models" on the basis of which other schools can be reformed, reorganized or restructured. For example, it was already said in 1924 of German experimental schools: "They must be germ-cells for the restructuring of our whole school system!"[73] Thus the "Kollegschulversuch" in North Rhine Westphalia was "expressly planned as a model for a future standard system." In this sense one also speaks of the "Kollegschule as a model for an integrated secondary level II."[74]

Also in this sense "model" means not a replica, but rather an "original." It refers to an "original," in the sense of "prototype," which serves as a *trial example* according to which many other educational institutions of a certain type will perhaps subsequently be established.

"Model" as Plan

Educators who want to educate in a rationally purposeful manner, and thereby teachers who wish to instruct with prospects of success, must first make plans. A *plan* is "a detailed scheme, program, or method worked out beforehand for the accomplishment of an object."[75]

In instruction specific teaching contents are to be transmitted within the limits of specific periods of time. Various large substantive parts of the structured teaching material, so-called teaching units, must be planned for time units of varying length. Of these, the systematically most important is the "annual content unit." The smallest, but methodically most important, is the "lesson unit," that is, that part of the learning material which is to be transmitted in a single lesson. One also speaks of the "subject unit."[76]

A concrete working plan, program or scheme for individual lessons is usually called an outline, schedule or lesson plan.[77] It is put down in writing and assists a teacher's individual preparation. More recently, lesson plans have frequently been called "*lesson models*" or "*instructional models*."[78] The process of developing a plan for instruction during a lesson, or an outline for instruction over longer time periods, is often called "*model construction*," "*model building*," "*model development*" or "*modelling*."[79] In the past, to the contrary, one used the entirely adequate terms (material and methodical) "preparation" or "preparing."[80]

As standardized guides or aids for teachers' individual

lesson preparation there have long been subject-level, school-level and method-specific sample plans, in the past called "instructional examples,"[81] "instructional patterns," "sample lessons" or "specimens." Today such aids are often also called "*instructional models.*" As an example we can use the following statements: "Instructional models are understood here as instruments for the planning, preparation, construction and realization of instructional processes. These instruments assist us in anticipating instructional processes."[82] Thus it is a matter of "models of instructional preparation" or "*preparation models.*"[83]

These planning aids for teachers, which are directly oriented to instructional practice, are also called "*didactic models.*" In them "specific possible combinations of teaching aims, instructional contents and methods are presented for critical reflection."[84]

The word "model," in the sense of "plan," is, however, employed not only in instructional theory, but also in the theory of educational organization and the language of educational politics. In these contexts one speaks of "*school models,*" especially of "school organizational *reform models,*" such as the "comprehensive school model,"[85] the "model of a new secondary school,"[86] "mobile instruction as an organizational model,"[87] etc. The realization of such plans is sometimes called "*model implementation.*"[88]

As well, drafts or guidelines for the organization of professional training and further training, which were once appropriately called "plans," have in recent years become "models." Examples of this are "basic models of school practice studies" (such as the "Berlin basic model"[89]) or the "structural model for teacher training and teacher further training in Baden-Württemberg."[90] The production of these "models" was, incidentally, not called simply "planning," but rather "*model planning.*" One need only, with objective correctness, replace the word "model" with the word "plan" to recognize that the expression "model planning" is just as redundant here as the neologism "plan planning."

Also in this sense the word "model" refers not to a copy of an original, but rather to a plan as a design or scheme worked out in advance which can be realized with a greater or lesser degree of faithfulness to the original, or may, to the contrary, go unrealized.

"Model" as Trial

In many cases the meaning of the word "model" in pedagogical texts becomes clear only if one replaces "model" with "trial." This applies especially for expressions like "model project," "model program," "model conditions," "model planning," "model completion," "model accompanying research," etc.

As an illustration we can make such substitutions in phrases from texts on the "Model Project Day-Mother."[91] These deal with trial arrangements for children to be cared for by substitute "mothers" while their real mothers are at work.

A "project" is a "plan or proposal; scheme" or "undertaking requiring concerted effort."[92] After substitution, a "model project" is seen to be no more than a "trial project," "trial plan," "trial proposal" or "trial undertaking." A "model program" is a "trial program." "Model conditions" are "trial conditions." "Factors involved in the model" are "factors involved in the trial." "Model planning" is "trial planning." "Children involved in the model" are involved in a trial. "Scientists taking part in the model" are taking part in a trial. "Model accompanying research" means "trial accompanying research"; "model implementation," "trial implementation."

The term "model trial"[93] means in this context "trial trial," which makes it especially apparent how redundant it is to speak of a "model" when one means a "trial."

"Model" as Category, Class, Type

By "category" is meant here a "class or division in a scheme of classification," species or sort of object. Also common is the word "type," which refers (among other things) to a category, species, "kind, class or group having distinguishing characteristics in common."[94]

For example, the word "model" is used with this sense in expressions such as the following: "models of pedagogical theory construction,"[95] "models of fundamental didactic theories,"[96] "major models of new didactic theories,"[97] "models of social pedagogical theory construction,"[98] "basic models of curriculum reform,"[99] "stationary models" and "alternative models of youth assistance,"[100] "models of cooperation with the educational industry,"[101] etc.

In all these cases "model" refers to nothing other than a species or class of a genus which differs through the common attributes of its members from other classes of the same genus. For example, an article on "Models of Pedagogical Theory Construction" ("Modelle pädagogischer Theorienbildung," Blass 1978), differentiates characteristic "positions of pedagogical theory construction" or types of "theory conceptions."[102] A book entitled *Models of Fundamental Didactic Theories* (Modelle grundlegender didaktischer Theorien, Ruprecht et al. 1972) deals with typical "conceptions" or "approaches" of general didactics.[103] In a book entitled *Institutional Education. Stationary Models and Alternatives* (Heimerziehung. Stationäre Modelle und Alternativen, Colla 1981) "phenomena of stationary educational assistance," thus types of reformatories, and various types of "cooperative living arrangements" are presented as alternatives for youth assistance. The article "Models of Cooperation with the Educational Industry" ("Modelle der Zusammenarbeit mit der Bildungsindustrie," Klotz 1975) discusses different "forms of cooperation" and "model types of cooperation with radio stations."[104] ("Model types" thus means here something like "form forms," "type types" or "sort sorts," insofar as the author consistently uses the word "model" in the sense of "form," which he seems to intend.) The genus is called, in the first text, "pedagogical theory"; in the second text, "didactic theory"; in the third text, "stationary educational assistance" or "institution for substitute education";[105] in the fourth text, "cooperation with radio stations."

The employment of the word "model" in place of "category," "class" or "type" is especially confusing when the things classified are themselves called "models," and authors or readers fail to see that the word "model" then stands for two completely different concepts. This confusion is apparent, for example, in texts on "models of didactic theories" in which individual theories are also called "models." One reads of a "didactic model," or specific "didactic models" or "models of didactics," where "theories" are meant, and of "model approaches," where it is a matter of "theoretical approaches."[106] Such "models" of "didactic models" are nothing else but categories (sorts, types or forms) of didactic theory.

In the sense of "category" the concept of "model" relates to classificatory schemes and does not have anything at all to do with a relation to or "depiction" of an "original."

"Model" as Leading Idea, Guiding Image or Image of Man

The author of a book on *Models of Pedagogical Understanding* (Modelle pädagogischen Verstehens, Loch 1978) described models as follows: they "are *guiding images* for thinking about relationships between people in educational situations." He also characterizes "models" as "thought structures" or "conceptions," and by nature as "simplifying and one-sided, temporary and therefore constantly in need of revision for understanding reality."[107] Presumably he means an outline of a theory, a mini-theory or a "theoruncula."[108] The author further claims that the manner in which a person "feels and experiences his world depends on the optimistic or pessimistic model through which he understands himself in his life world." Accordingly, a "model," understood as a "leading idea," must also have the sense "image of man."

The sense of "model" as an "image of man" is also found in an essay on "Psychological Models for Guidance" (Allport 1962). The author expressly understands the concept of "model" as meaning "a certain image of the nature of man" and the call is made "to find a more adequate image of man."[109]

"Model" as Paragon, Example or Exemplar

This sense is probably meant by book titles like *Comprehensive School. Model for the School of Tomorrow?* (Gesamtschule. Modell für die Schule von morgen? Magdeburg 1967)[110] or *Models of Modern Educational Policy* (Modelle moderner Bildungspolitik, Evers 1969).[111] In English texts we also find the expressions "model teacher" and "model lesson" used to designate an exemplary teacher or lesson suitable as a standard for the evaluation of other teachers or lessons.[112]

"Model" as World in Miniature

The following "thesis about the school as a model form of society" can serve as an example of this sense: "The *school*, as a *model of the society* in which coming generations will live, must, in an elementary and experienceable form, contain the very dangers and opportunities of this society: It must enable students to learn what society is *from* the school (instead of the way it has previously been attempted: *in* the school)."[113] Model thus means in this case a segment of reality (or environment) which is either (a) presumably similar to a larger overall reality or (b) ought to be made similar to one.

"Model" as Idea, Conception, Notion

In cybernetics and information theory it is usual to speak of the "internal model of the external world."[114] In psychology those contents of consciousness which contain information about the external world are called conceptions. Conceptions can be visual or non-visual. The word "thought" is usually employed in reference to primarily non-visual conceptions, ranging from image-poor (but still visualizable) conceptions to others that cannot be visualized at all.[115] Authors who advocate a model concept as content-poor and extensive as that preferred by the supporters of epistemological "modelism" (or of "universal model theory") also refer, among other things, to a person's subjective knowledge as a "model" ("internal model," "perceptual model," "cogitative model"[116]).

This usage of the word "model" has also found its way into didactic texts. What was previously called, in a perfectly clear manner, a "conception" or "thought" is today a "model" or "*model conception*."

In this sense, for example, it is asserted that "the central category of school didactics is the 'model.' Models are exemplary conceptions." "The conceptions whose furtherance is the chief task incumbent on the school acquire 'order' to the degree that they assume model character." "In the school [students] must learn to keep conceptions in consciousness long enough for them to take on the role of models. . . . Learning to think in models is the central didactic task of the school." Here partly fantastic, partly quite banal contributions are ascribed to models: "Models are an opportunity to visualize the unimaginable" (meant is probably the non-visual); on the other hand: "Models are thought bridges between the past and the future." But other than in the form of conceptions or thoughts there naturally are no such "bridges." These speculations reach a climax in the assertion that another pedagogical author "certainly is right when he says that what retards the future is the inability of most people to deal with models."[117]

However, back to serious analysis. It has been self-evident ever since Herbart that in instruction teachers should draw on the pupil's "range of thoughts." A child's chance experiences clearly do lead to the development of vast numbers of conceptions, but if children are left to themselves, they often acquire only a "chaotic apprehension" of things and events. Therefore instruction must include "analyses of experience, of facts learned in school, and of opinions," a process in which "the pupil's own thoughts are expressed first, and these thoughts, such as they chance to be, are then, with the teacher's help, analyzed, corrected, and supplemented." The "store of experiences which they bring with them must be worked over" in order to clarify their conceptions. New conceptions arise from this "thinking through of concepts."[118]

A contemporary admirer of model terminology has formulated a similar program as follows: "An introduction to be presented using instructional means to the development and use of models for the purposes of reconstruction (i.e., of playful copying) of reality (under the condition of specifiable interests)" is "to be described as a process of increasing formalization of trivial model conceptions into ever more specific or respectively more comprehensive structures which will be available as all-purpose instruments for the accounting and management of reality. So viewed, the task of instruction, above all in the elementary school, is to make in the structuralistic play of a didactic tinkering the 'models of the first order' of everyday life into guiding instruments."[119]

Some authors claim that this model concept also refers to an "original," "but under certain circumstances to an original which exists nowhere."[120] This statement could only make sense if one interpreted it in such a way that by "original" was intended a different "model" corresponding to nothing in extrapsychic reality. But naturally this model "exists" in human consciousness and can be objectified using language or other symbolic means. Because of the ambiguous statements made by the cited authors about their "model conceptions," there are no unequivocal answers to questions concerning the possibility of models with still unrealized originals. The only thing we can be sure of is that some human conceptions correspond in a fairly accurate way to empirical phenomena in the external world, while others, to the contrary, are personally created mixtures of memories and fancies. These latter conceptions correspond to no "original," but rather are themselves "original."

"Model" as Paradigm

In a study of "Contemporary Models of Teaching" (Nuthall and Snook 1973) the word "model" is used in the sense of "interpretive framework"[121] or "point of view," and specific reference is made to Thomas Kuhn,[122] who employs the expression "paradigm" for this. The "behavior-control model," the "discovery-learning model" and the "rational model" are dealt with as three "competing alternatives" for approaching instructional actions. "Each of these models consists of a set of associated ideas and concepts more or less organized around a larger conception of what teaching ought to be like, and how it ought to be viewed." Every researcher thinks "within the context of a model." The "model serves to simplify and organize the process of research"; it also "provides the grounds for interpreting and generalizing the empirical data which are obtained."[123]

In contrast to theories, the validity of such "models" can in no manner be empirically confirmed. One cannot even prove the superiority of one "model" to another. "Models" precede research, and the advocates of different models do not agree on the nature of useful research. "Each model is fundamentally a claim about how teaching *ought* to be understood and interpreted."[124]

Nor are the texts any clearer in which "models" are understood as "points of view." Thus, for example, we read that "theory models" can be divided into mechanistic and organismic "points of view" and that "educational research has been governed by mechanistic theory models." "Educational theory models" are thus "ideas to be represented in ideas representing educational states of affairs."[125] All that we can infer from this is that a "model" in this sense of the word precedes a theory, and that the theory is thought of as proceeding from the model. Thus the expression: "model or point of view from which the wanted theory can arise."

In view of these vague utterances, even referring back to Kuhn's sense of the word "paradigm" does not help, for the latter employs his term in at least twenty-one different senses.[126] In essence he appears to mean a "crude analogy" and therefore "a logically unknown entity."[127]

"Model" as Theory

By a "theory" in the broad sense of the word is understood a system of statements which contain more or less confirmed knowledge of a specific subject area.[128] Scientific work consists chiefly in creating testable theories and in their empirical testing.[129]

Many of the things which have been called "models" in recent pedagogical texts are nothing other than theories, be they scientific or practical. The following definition from an essay on "The Function of Models in Didactic Theory" ("Die Funktion von Modellen in der didaktischen Theorie," Popp 1970) can serve as an example of the sense of "model" as a "scientific theory of instruction":[130] "A model is a logically consistent system of hypotheses (axioms, deductions, prognoses) which are understood as in principle needing verification—it is a provisional construct." As a further clarification the author also states that: "In a model a complicated, incomprehensible constellation is reduced to a few significant features and basic structures which first become visible and accessible to scientific study through reduction. The excluded factors are thereby not denied; for methodical reasons they are merely temporarily or essentially left out of consideration."[131]

These and many similar statements leave it unclear how a model in the sense intended by the author differs from a theory. Rather, all the attributes with which he defines his model concept are also found in the definition of a scientific theory. Thus he merely uses a new term in the place of a familiar term. This conclusion also holds for Mader's "model of personality development and personality formation":[132] it displays all the attributes of a theory.

Many pedagogical authors, it should be added, appear blissfully unaware that they are employing the term "model" synonymously with the concept of theory. Otherwise they would hardly use expressions like "model theory of didactics" or "model character of different theoretical approaches,"[133] because "theory theory of didactics" (i.e., of the *theory* of instruction) and other redundant expressions are all too easily recognized as nonsense.

The employment of the ambiguous term "model" in addition to and in place of the term "theory" is also found in a book entitled *Theories and Models of Didactics* (Theorien und Modelle der Didaktik, Blankertz 1975).[134] "Model" in this text is nothing more than another word for "theory." The "individual models" discussed by the author are in fact simply "didactic theories."[135] If the title were instead *Theories of Didactics*, its informational content would be no less.[136] A further example is offered by a book on *The Structural Model of Didactics* (Das Strukturmodell der Didaktik, Glogauer 1967). Despite the title, it contains in essence merely a structural theory of the "didactic problem field."[137]

As already mentioned, in this context it is not a matter of using the term "model" to differentiate between scientific and practical theories of education.[138] In fact, the term "model" is employed for both types of educational theory. Especially often, however, it is indeed *practical theories* of instruction that are designated as models. Thus we read, for example, of a "model of instructional planning." "This model should help us to so understand school instruction as a social action field, that it becomes easier for those acting in this field to agree on the planning elements of their action, to test the effectiveness of planning," etc.[139]

The following explanation is offered in an American text on *Social Models of Teaching* (Weil and Joyce 1978): "A model of teaching consists of guidelines for designing educational activities and environments. It specifies ways of teaching and learning that are intended to achieve certain kinds of goals. A model includes a rationale, a theory that justifies it and describes what it is good for and why; the rationale may be accompanied by empirical evidence that it 'works'." It is a practical theory based on scientific theories: "on defendable theories about how people learn, grow, and develop."[140]

In the same sense, the "Gießen Didactic Model"[141] is also a practical theory. "Didactic models assist respectively planning and analyzing instruction; they are *instructions for action* (norms) which indicate to the teacher how he should respectively plan and analyze instruction."[142] "Instructional models state rules"; "they provide impetus for practicable instructional planning."[143]

Sometimes, we should note, it is hard to tell whether the expression "didactic model" means a scientific theory *of* instruction or a practical theory *for* (future) instruction, because the definition is stated in such a way that it seems to vindicate both senses.[144]

That it is at any rate a matter of a theory can easily be established merely by replacing the word "model" in the text with the word "theory," whereby no change in meaning occurs, but only a clarification. Some authors even make such substitutions.[145]

Those authors who use the term "model" in the sense of "theory" fail to clearly define the relationship between "original" and "replica." Anyone who means a *practical* theory advocates a "not only, but also" viewpoint—depending on the function of the "model." If it is based on earlier descriptions of instructional reality, it is a "replica" or "copy"; if it is a proposed design for future instruction, it is an "original," pattern or "Urbild." Of course the view is also advocated that a theory intended to be employed in planning (as an "action or planning model") is not an original, but to the contrary, something whose "original ought to be realized in the *future*."[146]

"Model" as Empirical Theory as Far as It Serves as an Example for an Empirical Theory of a Different Subject Area

Some educational theorists are of the opinion that the design and improvement of empirical theories of education can be furthered by patterning them after theories about other subject areas. Both empirical and formal sciences can be employed thereby.[147] These authors believe in the possibility of "theory construction in which one theory becomes a *model for* another theory."[148]

Outside the formal disciplines of logic and mathematics, for this purpose it is chiefly the natural and social sciences that come into consideration. Thus, for example, attempts have been made to use general systems theory, agricultural economics, pharmacology or even quantum theory as "models" for educational theories.[149] With the exception of systems theory, it has not been possible to demonstrate the fruitfulness of doing so. Furthermore, analogies between agriculture, the use of medication or the movements of particles, on the one hand, and educational phenomena, on the other, are too vague. They go no further than a listing of superficial similarities from which no new educational science hypotheses can be derived.[150]

Likewise in this sense a "model" is not a "replica," but rather an "original."

"Model" as a Mathematical Theory as Far as It Serves as an Example for the Design of Hypotheses Belonging to an Empirical Theory

The word "model" is also employed in educational research to refer to a mathematical theory used for the formulation or improvement of an empirical theory. The supposition that it could be useful for the acquisition of empirical knowledge (or have heuristic value) is based on the assumption of a degree of structural similarity between the cases which the theory has been shown to explain and phenomena which are yet to be studied. Obviously this presupposes the prior existence of a provisional empirical theory of these phenomena.

We can take as an example the studies of educators' behavior in which so-called "instrumentality theory," (a type of "expectancy-value theory")[151] is adopted as a "model." The task in such studies is to formulate an empirical theory about the educational behavior being studied that is structurally similar to (or isomorphic with) the purely formal theory used as a model. Then it must be empirically tested whether educators actually behave in accord with the predictions of the empirical theory formulated to explain their behavior.[152] If that should prove the case, the laws stated by the formal theory (model) can be used to generate new empirical hypotheses about the educational behavior being studied. Additional empirical testing will then be required to determine whether the new hypotheses do in fact hold for the educational phenomena to be explained. If so the model will have shown its usefulness as an aid to educational research.

Also in this context a "model" is not a replica or copy, but rather an "original," a theory which serves as a pattern for the construction of another theory.

"Model" as Partial Draft of a Theory

Sometimes the expression "model" also means an intermediate product in the process of theory construction, be it a conceptual framework or a hypothesis. As an example we can use an essay entitled "A model of school learning" (Carroll 1963), in which the author discusses a "conceptual model." He refers specifically to "a schematic design or conceptual model of factors affecting success in school learning and of the way they interact" and in addition uses the term "framework" for this. "Such a model should use a very small number of simplifying concepts, conceptually independent of one another and referring to phenomena at the same level of discourse."[153] His "model says that the learner will succeed in learning a given task to the extent that he spends the amount of time that he needs to learn the task."[154] He is thus using the term model in the sense of a hypothesis, as part of a theory.

Besides several other model concepts, another author, Aschersleben, also employs this model concept: "Models are first steps for theories"; "didactic models" are thus "first steps for didactic theories."[155] He refers to "didactic models" as "theory-like representations of instructional reality" which should offer "initial orientation aid."

OUTLINE OF A CRITIQUE AND PROSPECTS

I began with the fact that in recent years the word "model" has become common in pedagogics. Thereby the impression is widespread that it has a single, clearly defined sense, one which is generally known and accepted. This impression is mistaken. My analysis of German and English language pedagogical texts has, rather, shown the following:

1. The word "model" is employed in at least fifteen often quite different senses. Instead of a single generally accepted model concept, contemporary pedagogics has at least fifteen different model concepts. Still further model concepts exist in other sciences which up to now have still not found their way into pedagogics. The most noteworthy example is the concept of model as a "formalized representation of an empirical theory." It is, among other things, already common in psychology and will in the future probably find supporters in the empirical science of education.

2. Many of the model concepts employed in pedagogics are inadequately defined. In some cases the word "model" appears to be used only as a pretentious pseudo-scientific term, a decorative fashion word lacking specific conceptual contents. There are also pedagogical texts in which the intended sense of the word "model" cannot be inferred, even from the context.

In view of its ambiguity, one must decide whether to make any future use of the word "model"—and if so, in what sense.

I regard it as fruitless to construct a model concept which is so general that it can be applied to all or at least most things which today are called "models." Even if this were possible—in view of the results of Stachowiak's attempt to develop a universal essentialistic definition, I greatly doubt this—such a model concept would be so poor in contents that it could serve no practical purpose.

Presupposing the above, only one possibility remains:

to examine whether among the above described fifteen senses of the word "model" there is one sense, or whether a combined sense can be created from several common senses, which cannot be better designated by a term other than "model."

In my opinion, this is not the case with the four senses in which the word "model" means theory. Anyone who says "model" instead of "theory" only duplicates vocabulary. As a synonym for "theory" the word "model" creates redundant terminology and is thus superfluous.

The same holds for senses five through eleven: trial, category, leading idea, paragon, example or exemplar, world in miniature, idea or conception and paradigm.

This leaves only four possible senses: "model" as teaching means, as object of imitation, as prototype and as plan.

Of these it seems to me that the first sense (teaching means) is the most common in pedagogical language and the least easily replaced by another word. The chief attribute of this model concept is "copy" (or "replica"). In the second sense (object of imitation), the third sense (prototype) and the fourth sense (plan), the chief attribute is, to the contrary, "original" (or "Urbild").

An unambiguous model concept can only be created if one either decides for the attribute "copy" or "replica," or for the attribute "original." A "model *of* something" is, despite the shared term "model," objectively quite different from a "model *for* something." The one is a copy or *replica of something already in existence*, the other, a *pattern, plan or design for something yet to be created*. With a replica the similarity to the original (and thereby the truth value) can in principle always be tested. If, to the contrary, "model" means an original, then quite different and much more complicated problems of testing arise, insofar as the original is a prototype or plan. One problem is to decide what a model should be compared with—its copy or its source. It is reasonable that originals of this sort should not first be compared with their replicas—thus in the case of a plan, with the results of attempts to realize it—but with knowledge of reality which is already available at the time the original is created and whose creation it co-determines. This, however, is not unproblematic, as explained below.

Because of the factual, epistemological and methodological differences between an original and a replica, I am of the view that the name "model" should not be used for *both*. Faced with a choice, it seems to me that there are more reasons for associating the term "model" with the concept of "replica" than with that of "original" (respectively the "Urbild" or "ideal"). The chief reason for this is that the attribute of similarity which belongs to the basic meaning of the word "model" presupposes the existence of a replica similar to an original. An original can, to the contrary, exist without a replica, a plan without execution, an ideal without realization, and thereby also without the relationship of similarity as an essential conceptual attribute. My proposal for the use of the word "model" is also consistent with one of Stachowiak's conclusions. Based on his semantic analysis, he decided that the most important feature of a "universal model concept" is the "replication attribute": "Models are always models *of something*." "Models have a replication function."[156]

Thereby I am also against the employment of senses two, three and four. Only the first sense remains: "model" as a teaching aid for the illustration or clarification of an "original." This means that of the fifteen senses of the word "model" currently employed in pedagogics, I regard fourteen to be superfluous. "Model" is a fashionable word whose uncritical adoption in pedagogics has hindered clarity of thinking on the part of educational theorists and educational practitioners far more than it has helped.

NOTES

1. On the problems of concept formation and the process of conceptual explication cf. BREZINKA (1994: 14 ff. and 23 ff.).

2. AYTO (1990: 351); *Oxford Latin Dictionary* (1968: 1124).

3. *Revised Medieval Latin Word-List* (1983: 302).

4. PARTRIDGE (1966: 411); *Barnhart Dictionary of Etymology* (1988: 670). German etymology in GRIMM (1962: col. 2439); R. MÜLLER (1980: 205). In Old High German the word "modul" was used, which in Middle High German became "model" (with the accent on the first syllable). In the sixteenth century this word was replaced by the word "Modell," borrowed from the Italian "modello" and French forms.

5. AYTO (1990: 351).

6. *Oxford English Dictionary*, 2nd ed. (1989, Vol. 9: 940 ff.).

7. *Oxford English Dictionary*, 2nd ed. (1989, Vol. 9: 941).

8. *American Heritage Dictionary*, 2nd ed. (1982: 806). R. MÜLLER (1980); *Meyer* (1976); *Brockhaus* (1971: 678); *Duden* (1978: 1805).

9. *Longman Dictionary of Contemporary English* (1987: 668).

10. *Oxford English Dictionary*, 2nd ed. (1989, Vol. 9: 942).

11. *Duden* (1978: 1805); CHAO (1962: 559); R. MÜLLER (1980: 203). *Oxford English Dictionary*, 2nd ed. (1989, Vol. 9: 942): "serving or intended to serve as a model; suited to be a model, exemplary, ideally perfect."

12. G. FREY (1961: 89).

13. Cf. G. FREY (1961: 90 ff.); JAMMER (1965); STOFF (1969: 52 ff.); STRAASS (1963); USCHMANN (1968); R. MÜLLER (1980: 213 ff.).

14. SCHÜRMANN (1977: 106).

15. *Oxford English Dictionary*, 2nd ed. (1989, Vol. 9: 940 ff.).

16. Cf. *inter alia* BOMBACH (1965); KRECH and KLEIN

(1952); METZGER (1965); MAYNTZ (1967); TACK (1969); K. DEUTSCH (1963); CHAO (1962); P. HARTMANN (1965); SCHWEIZER (1980).

17. Cf. *inter alia* BRODBECK (1968); FREUDENTHAL (1961); BRAITHWAITE (1962); STOFF (1969); STACHOWIAK (1965, 1973 and 1983); HESSE (1966 and 1967); SPINNER (1973); BUNGE (1973); WARTOFSKY (1979).

18. KAPLAN (1964: 258); similar WENDLER (1965: 284); SCHÜRMANN (1977: 106); SCHMIDT (1980: 162 f.).

19. CHAO (1962: 563).

20. Cf. APOSTEL (1961: 1); BRODBECK (1968); NAGEL (1961: 108 ff.); STEGMÜLLER (1969, Vol. 1: 133 ff.).

21. Cf. STACHOWIAK (1965: 437 ff. and 1973: 131 ff.).

22. STACHOWIAK (1965: 438).

23. STACHOWIAK (1973: 131 ff.). Emphasis in the original. Similar: STACHOWIAK (1965: 438 and 1980: 29).

24. STACHOWIAK (1980a: 41 f.).

25. Cf. STACHOWIAK (1973: 56 ff.).

26. Cf., e.g., APOSTEL (1961: 36 f.).

27. Of course, because STACHOWIAK is also aware of this he attaches great importance to the differentiation of "model types" and their definition.

28. Cf. STOFF (1969: 23 ff.).

29. STOFF (1969: 32).

30. Cf. KLAUS and BUHR (1975: 63); KONDAKOW (1978: 27).

31. KLAUS and BUHR (1975: 810).

32. KONDAKOW (1978: 351 f.).

33. KLAUS and BUHR (1975: 805).

34. KLAUS and BUHR (1975: 808); similar is CLAUSS (1976: 347).

35. Cf., e.g., KAHN (1977).

36. BRODBECK (1968: 583).

37. STEGMÜLLER (1969, Vol. 1: 133 ff.). On the value of isomorphism for the methodology of the sciences cf. KLAUS and BUHR (1975: 588).

38. Cf., e.g., POSCH (1967: 75 ff.).

39. PITTIONI (1983).

40. TARSKI (1971: 11). *Oxford English Dictionary*, 2nd ed. (1989, Vol. 9: 941): In mathematical logic a model is

"a set of entities that satisfies all the formulas of a given formal or axiomatic system."

41. G. MÜLLER (1965: 158) (with a detailed explication and justification of this definition).

42. For example, SUPPES (1969: 12). Because of the (still) lacking prerequisites for the application of the mathematical concept of model in the empirical sciences, G. MÜLLER (1965: 164 ff.) is much more reserved.

43. STACHOWIAK (1973: 4).

44. Cf. BREZINKA (1992).

45. CHAPANIS (1961: 115 f.).

46. G. FREY (1961: 94).

47. SCHILLER and LINDNER (1906: 35); HEUMANN (1966: 344); AEBLI (1976: 128).

48. So already ZILLER (1876: 271); for experimental evidence cf. DÜKER and TAUSCH (1957). Cf. R. MAYER (1989) on models and instructional techniques.

49. ASCHERSLEBEN and HOHMANN (1979: 19).

50. Cf. THIEL (1976: 24 ff.).

51. Many further schemas from didactics in MEMMERT (1977).

52. E.g., NEUGEBAUER (1980: 58 ff.).

53. Cf., e.g., K. SCHNEIDER (1978: 152).

54. C.G. SALZMANN (1780: 93).

55. Cf., e.g., REIN (1895).

56. The term "model" for the "object of imitation" was of course occasionally used already in the nineteenth century, e.g., by SAILER (1822), who admonished educators: "See to it that the earliest surroundings of the pupil are as much as possible perfect models. . . . But of all that surrounds the pupil, be yourself the most perfect of all models which shape him, be the best" (p. 79).

57. Cf. BANDURA and WALTERS (1963); BANDURA (1971).

58. KLAUSMEIER and RIPPLE (1973: 69).

59. TAUSCH (1977: 46) (corresponding to the term "perceptual learning," as opposed to "imitative learning").

60. KLAUSMEIER and RIPPLE (1975: 37).

61. *American Heritage Dictionary*, 2nd ed. (1982: 997).

62. *American Heritage Dictionary*, 2nd ed. (1982:

997): From the Greek "protos," meaning first and "tupos," meaning model.

63. K. SCHNEIDER (1978: 149).

64. Cf., e.g., W. FLITNER (1954 and 1956); HENTIG (1965: 51); A. FLITNER (1968); AURIN (1972: 20 ff.).

65. Cf., e.g., DEISSLER (1978); WINKELMANN (1977).

66. Cf., e.g., KEUCHEL (1983).

67. The heading most frequently applied to "model" in the *Bibliographie Pädagogik* (1978, Vol. 13: p. 818). Cf. BLANKERTZ (1977).

68. HENTIG (1965: 51 f.).

69. HEHLMANN (1971: 377).

70. W. FLITNER (1954a: 135).

71. ODENBACH (1974: 325) (my italics). According to W. FLITNER (1954: 137) "model schools" should be and set "examples of internal reform."

72. GLÄSS and KLAFKI (1961: col. 873).

73. HILKER (1924: 448); similar on the newer German model schools AURIN (1972: 22).

74. BLANKERTZ (1977: 178 and 194).

75. *American Heritage Dictionary*, 2nd ed. (1982: 947). On planning in the educational domain cf. DOLCH (1962).

76. MEISTER (1947: 158). German: "Stundeneinheit," "Lehrstück."

77. MEISTER (1947: 162); K. SCHNEIDER (1978: 156). Equivalent German terms: "Stundenbild," "Stundenbildschema," "Planungsschema" or "Unterrichtsentwurf."

78. German: "Stundenbildmodelle" or "Unterrichtsmodelle." Cf., e.g., MÖLLER (1966: 13 and 23).

79. Cf., e.g., SALZMANN and KOHLBERG (1983). German: "Modellkonstruktion," "Modellbildung," "Modellentwicklung" or "Modellierung."

80. Cf. MARTINAK (1908).

81. Cf. DIETRICH (1969). German: "Unterrichtsbeispiele," "Unterrichtsmuster," "Musterlektionen" or "Präparationen."

82. NESTLE (1975: 172).

83. K. SCHNEIDER (1978: 146). German: "Modelle der Unterrichtsvorbereitung," "Vorbereitungsmodelle."

84. HILLER (1973: 213).

85. Cf., e.g., RAUSCHENBERGER (1975).

86. STRAUBE (1966). Here the German "Gymnasium."

87. STRAUBE (1966: 20 ff.). German: "beweglicher Unterricht."

88. WINKELMANN (1977: 75).

89. DIETRICH/ELZER/FRANK/MALSCH (1972: 35 ff.). German: "Berliner Grundmodell." This was a 1972 plan for an integrated system of teacher training.

90. KULTUSMINISTERIUM (1968). Baden-Württemberg is a state in southwestern Germany.

91. Cf. HASSENSTEIN (1974); PETTINGER (1974); KREUZER (1978).

92. *American Heritage Dictionary*, 2nd ed. (1982: 990).

93. German: "Modellversuch." HASSENSTEIN (1974: 425).

94. *Webster's New World Dictionary* (1988: 221, 1446).

95. BLASS (1978).

96. RUPRECHT/BECKMANN/CUBE/SCHULZ (1972).

97. RUPRECHT/BECKMANN/CUBE/SCHULZ (1972: 9).

98. WOLLENWEBER (1981).

99. K. FREY (1975, Vol. 1: 257 ff.).

100. COLLA (1981).

101. G. KLOTZ (1975).

102. BLASS (1978, Vol. 1: 10; Vol. 2: 12).

103. RUPRECHT/BECKMANN/CUBE/SCHULZ (1972).

104. G. KLOTZ (1975: 144).

105. COLLA (1981: 13).

106. Especially apparent with RUPRECHT/BECKMANN/CUBE/SCHULZ (1972: 9 ff.).

107. LOCH (1978: 7).

108. BRAITHWAITE (1962: 225).

109. ALLPORT (1962: 373 and 381).

110. MAGDEBURG (1967).

111. EVERS (1969).

112. NUTHALL and SNOOK (1973: 47).

113. HENTIG (1968: 13) (my italics); on p. 65 "education" is even called on to "make itself a model of this

society."

114. STEINBUCH (1971: 134). For a critique cf. NICKLIS (1967: 134 ff.).

115. ROHRACHER (1963: 249 ff.).

116. STACHOWIAK (1965: 446 ff.).

117. WILHELM (1969: 296 and 305 ff.). The cited author is HENTIG (1964: 174).

118. HERBART (1977: 106 ff.-§§ 110, 106, 112 and 1913, Vol. 1: 309 ff.). Also: "Instruction builds on the pupil's experience."

119. HILLER (1976: 145).

120. WILHELM (1969: 307).

121. POLANYI (1962: 97 ff.).

122. T. KUHN (1970).

123. NUTHALL and SNOOK (1973: 48 f.).

124. NUTHALL and SNOOK (1973: 50).

125. STEINER (1978: 18 ff.).

126. Cf. MASTERMAN (1970: 61 ff.).

127. MASTERMAN (1970: 79 ff.).

128. Cf. BREZINKA (1992: 103 ff.).

129. Cf. POPPER (1964: 99 ff.).

130. POPP (1970: 50).

131. POPP (1970: 53).

132. MADER (1979: 151 ff.).

133. POPP (1970: 60).

134. BLANKERTZ (1975).

135. BLANKERTZ (1975: 7).

136. To be sure the title ought to be *Instructional Theories* or *Theories of Instruction*. Since "didactics" generally means "instructional *theory*" or "*theory* of instruction" (DOLCH 1965: 45), as also demonstrated by the book title *Didaktik als Bildungslehre* [*Didactics as Educational Theory*] chosen by WILLMANN (German: 1957; an English edition was published under a different title in 1930) and WENIGER (1960), "theories of didactics" really means "theories of instructional theory," thus "meta-theories" of instruction, which BLANKERTZ, however, cannot have meant. He deals, rather, with a few basic forms, types or categories of instructional theory.

137. GLOGAUER (1967).

138. Cf. BREZINKA (1992: 3 ff.).
139. W. SCHULZ (1980: 6 and 9).
140. WEIL and JOYCE (1978: 2).
141. HAIN and RICKER (1980). Gießen is a city in the state of Hessen, Germany.
142. E. KÖNIG (1980: 40). (Italics in original).
143. HILLER (1971: 275).
144. E.g., in SALZMANN (1974: 171).
145. Cf., e.g., SALZMANN and KOHLBERG (1983: 933): "every observation is always permeated by theories and particularly models."
146. SALZMANN (1975: 261).
147. Cf. STEINER-MACCIA/MACCIA/JEWETT (1963: 38 ff.).
148. STEINER (1981: 97).
149. Cf. STEINER-MACCIA/MACCIA/JEWETT (1963).
150. For a critique cf. JACOBSON/STIMART/WREN (1971).
151. KRAMPEN and BRANDSTÄDTER (1981).
152. Cf. STEGMÜLLER (1969, Vol. 1: 135).
153. CARROLL (1963: 723).
154. CARROLL (1963: 725). (Italics in original).
155. ASCHERSLEBEN (1983: 62 ff.).
156. SCHAEFER/TROMMER/WENK (1977: 210).

3

"Conflict Education": Analysis and Critique of a New Pedagogical Slogan

The language used by educators and educational theorists is always influenced by currently fashionable ideological and political orientations. We need only recall the events of the last few decades. Under the German National Socialist dictatorship (1933-45), German educators were expected to teach values such as those of the "Volksgemeinschaft" or national community, "obedience," "loyalty" and "self-sacrifice." Then, during the first twenty years of democratic reconstruction after 1945, emphasis was placed on education for "responsibility" and "partnership," thus on attitudes which further cooperation in a free and democratic society.

After West Germans had accustomed themselves to their new affluence, culturally critical intellectuals began around 1965 to have doubts about the existing societal order and to foment dissatisfaction with it. The New Left protest movement triggered an upsurge of radical societal and cultural critique which penetrated deep into so-called bourgeois society, into all political parties and even into the churches. This led to a change of consciousness with the result that subsequently the negative aspects of modern life situations and interpersonal relationships have been one-sidedly overemphasized. The new guiding ideas are "critique," "freedom from dominance," "emancipation," "ability for conflict." The societal image of the rebuilding phase after the Second World

War is now stigmatized, because it emphasized harmony, cooperation and partnership. In its place a so-called "*conflict model of society*" is propagated. Those who let themselves be guided by it are chiefly aware of abuses, misuse of power, oppression and conflict in the world. While in the old "*harmony model*" *of society* the shadow side was minimized, in the "conflict model" it is made the chief content of the image of societal reality.

Such a displacement in the interpretation of the world naturally influences the theory and praxis of education. We find a radical *revaluation of previous educational aims* and *propaganda* for *new educational aims*. The educational actions used to achieve these aims are called "*conflict education*." One of these new aims is so-called "*conflict ability*." The theory of "conflict education" is propagated under the name "*conflict pedagogics*." All these expressions are new.[1] Though introduced into pedagogical terminology only in the last few years, they have found widespread use among educators of various political and ideological orientations.

Since everyone knows that there are conflicts in the world, it is easy to accept the claim that children should be educationally prepared for conflict. This seems so convincing that there is a great danger of our too hastily and uncritically approving everything referred to by the new slogan "conflict education." Most do not realize how confused the underlying ideas are and how harmful they can be. One among many tasks assigned to philosophers of education is the critical examination of new slogans and the clarification of their meaning for other citizens. Only if one knows what they mean can one wisely decide for or against the matters which underlie them.

I would like in this essay to provide a clarification of the slogan "conflict education." What does it mean? What ideas lie behind it? On what assumptions about people, educational aims and the means to achieving these aims is it based? I will begin with an analysis of the meanings of the word and the views which are named with it. Following this I will give a few recommendations for a critique of these views, from both empirical and normative perspectives.

ANALYSIS OF THE TERMS INVOLVED

The new term "conflict pedagogics" is composed of two words which have long been familiar. The word "conflict" comes from the Latin "confligere," which means striking together, and "conflictus," meaning collision, hostile striking.[2] "Pedagogics" means an educational teaching, a theory of education, or more modestly: a system of statements about education.

In everyday language "conflict" has a variety of different senses, including among the most important "an encounter with arms," a "fight," "battle," "prolonged struggle"; "fighting," "contending with arms," "martial strife," "mental or spiritual struggle within a man," "the clashing or variance of opposed principles, statements, arguments," the "opposition, in an individual, of incompatible wishes or needs of approximately equal strength; also, the distressing emotional state resulting from such opposition," "dashing together, collision or violent mutual impact of physical bodies."[3]

If "pedagogics" is the theory of education, then "conflict pedagogics" would have to mean the theory of "*conflict education*." Such a theory, in the strict sense of the word, has not previously existed—neither as a scientific, nor even as a practical theory.[4] At present there are only opinions or views on conflict education which are far from being scientifically clarified, systematized and supported.

At any rate there is a term "conflict education" and its associated problems. It has already been the topic of articles in pedagogical dictionaries.[5] Generally understood, it means something like "resistance and/or opposition education." But what does this mean in particular? "Education for resistance and/or opposition?" Or more precisely: "for the ability to resist and oppose," "for the ability to engage in resistance and/or opposition?"

The word "conflict" would in this case relate to an *edu-*

cational aim: the psychic readiness or disposition to be able to resist and/or oppose. Antonius Wolf defines it in this sense as follows: "Conflict education means educating a person so that he becomes ready and able to engage in the conflicts which arise in the various areas of his environment, i.e., to confront them and not simply to eliminate them as mere disturbances in a strived-for equilibrium."[6] It is therefore a matter of being able to endure, bear, live with, hold out in or fight through conflicts. This educational aim is also expressed in short as "*conflict ability*."[7] If this aim is meant, then "conflict education" would mean "*education for conflict ability*,"[8] understood as the "ability" to live "in and with conflicts."[9]

However, a different educational aim could also be intended: the ability to avoid conflicts or to settle, resolve, arbitrate, negotiate, end or assuage them. I will call this educational aim for short "*conflict avoidance and settlement ability*" or "reconciliation ability." This aim is, for example, pursued for parental education by Thomas Gordon in his book *Parent Effectiveness Training*: the ability to resolve conflicts between parents and children.[10]

A third educational aim could, however, also be intended: the ability to cause, provoke, incite, bring forth and exploit conflicts in the pursuit of personal aims. One can call this for short "*conflict production and exploitation ability*." In this sense "conflict education" would thus be understood as "*education for causing and exploiting conflict*." Peter Brückner seems, for example, to have this sense in mind when he sets store by the "organization of the growing conflict and protest potential as a counterforce," or when he asserts that "peace can only come to us as *implacable*," i.e., that one "must renounce as unpeaceful the peace of oppression."[11]

This aim has central significance above all for supporters of so-called "revolutionary conflict research." They regard, among others, as well "strategies of polarization and of revolution" as "techniques for the resolution of conflict."[12] They polemicize against the "appeasement strategy of conflict resolution": "A fundamental conflict probably has first to be made manifest (which will probably, if not necessarily, end in a more or less violent confrontation) before it can be resolved."[13] One must "primarily develop means for abolishing (undermining, overthrowing) those structural power relations which are responsible for violence in order to subsequently reorganize the situation. This is nothing less than peace research with the aim of subversion and revolution, it becomes revolutionary research."[14] Essential for this program is the unusual concept of *violence* underlying it. "Violence" is seen as "not necessarily" something which "is visibly committed by someone against someone else." "Violence is present when the physical, material and/or mental status of a person is less than it could be on the basis of the influenceable factors in the given situation. Accordingly this means that someone loses value or is hindered in realizing *possible* values. This can happen as a result of visible *direct violence* by a consciously acting subject, but it can also be inherent in the circumstances": in some cases "no one in fact consciously performs 'acts of violence' against another person," but rather "violence" is "inherent in the structure of the situation itself" and is therefore called "*structural violence*."[15]

Finally, a fourth educational aim could be intended: knowledge of conflicts, understanding of conflicts; the ability to recognize, analyze and judge conflicts. "Conflict education" in this sense would therefore be "*education for knowledge about conflicts, for the ability to recognize, explain and judge conflicts.*" Something of the sort is meant for example by Lingelbach in an article on "conflict as a basic concept of political education": "The growing child should learn to recognize the greater conflicts which affect the entire society, to appropriately analyze and judge them."[16]

There are consequently at least four senses of the term "conflict education," insofar as the word "conflict" can be related to educational *aims*:

1. education for the ability to engage in conflicts,

2. education for the ability to avoid and resolve conflicts (reconciliation ability),
3. education for inciting and exploiting conflicts,
4. education for knowledge of conflicts, for the ability to know, explain and judge conflicts.

With the first three senses the aims focused on are dispositions for action, attitudes and opinions; with the fourth sense, the aims are knowledge and analytical-critical thinking ability. Obviously other senses of "conflict education" are also possible which would be defined by various combinations of the aim-attributes of these four concepts. Depending on which of these educational aims are pursued, a theory of conflict education, i.e., a "conflict pedagogics," has different contents.

But there is also an entirely different concept of "conflict education." This is one in which the word "conflict" is used not in reference to an educational *aim*, but rather to a *means* employed or recommended for achieving specific educational aims. "Conflict education" means in this case *"education through conflict"* or *"with the aid of conflict."* It is this concept which is, for example, intended by Klaus Mollenhauer when he speaks of the "educational function of conflicts" or considers their "educational meaning" and "the initiation of conflict situations and the introduction of a praxis for their settlement in the educational field."[17] The initiation of conflicts and their settlement are here regarded as means to achieving the educational aims of "maturity," "judiciousness" and "critical rationality."

The provisional result of this analysis of the meanings of the terms "conflict pedagogics" and "conflict education" is that they are *ambiguous*. We find not *one* or *the* concept of "conflict pedagogics," but several. Therefore with every contribution to this topic it is necessary to state which concept is respectively meant by the term "conflict pedagogics." This can be done. But much more problematic than the ambiguity of the term is the vagueness of all five concepts which I have found and differentiated. This arises because the component word "conflict" is itself employed in many senses, of which most are quite vague. They are vague concepts because they are not clearly defined and thus lack a precise meaning.

Conflict concepts are also among the substantively poorest general concepts that exist. Accordingly their extensions, i.e., the range of things which they comprehend, are very large. They include various classes of phenomena such as *psychic* (mental, intra-individual or intra-personal) conflicts, on the one hand, and inter-personal or *social* conflicts, on the other. The concept of *social conflict* comprehends such extremely varied phenomena as conflict between marital partners, siblings, pupils or neighbors, conflicts between parents and children, employers and employees, wage disputes between unions and employer organizations, distributional conflicts between interest groups and government, tensions between political parties, religious communities, peoples, races, states and blocs on up to and including war.

There is an extensive literature on the psychology,[18] as well as the sociology,[19] of conflict. It is, for example, held that man can be defined as "a conflict-prone being," that conflict is "the source and centerpiece of psychology";[20] that "not conflict and change, but stability and order are the pathological special case in life,"[21] etc. This means that conflict occurs everywhere and at all times, *in* people and their surroundings, nearby and far away; if not as visible, open or "manifest," then at least as "latent" conflict. Life means to live with and in conflict. Thereby the range of "conflict phenomena" ranges from the trivial, e.g., psychic motivational conflicts, such as the inability to decide whether to go to a movie or do homework, to domestic industrial conflict, social, racial or ethnic conflict, on up to international "conflicts" such as the Vietnam war, the civil wars in Yugoslavia and Afghanistan or the Arab-Israeli conflict.

Sympathetically expressed, one could say that "conflict," while to be sure poor in delimiting attributes, is nevertheless indispensable as a basic social science concept. But one can, to the contrary, reply that a number of major social scientists have emphasized other concepts, as for example Max Weber.[22] Expressed more critically one could say: "Conflict" is an extremely vague collective name, a fashionable slogan which is unusable for acquiring empirical knowledge, because it seduces us to view essentially different, disparate and incommensurable phenomena as similar in nature.[23]

As educationists we could leave the problems of conflict concepts to conflict researchers. But how can we explain with sufficient precision what, under these conditions, we should understand the term "conflict pedagogics" to mean? What phenomena do statements about "conflict education" refer to?

ANALYSIS OF THE BASIC THEORETICAL ASSUMPTIONS

As far as I can judge, at present there are only superficial, poorly developed and imprecise statements about "conflict education." These vary depending on the author's image of man, the aims pursued and the means. Common to them is, however, that almost always societal or *social conflicts* are meant, not psychic (or intra-personal) ones.

The Image of Man and Society

It is assumed by the advocates of a special "conflict education" that "the present and future situation of the individual in an industrialized, technological world and pluralistic society" requires a "life with conflict," "and at that not as the exception, but as the rule. Not conflict, but lack of conflict must appear as the doubtful, exceptional case."[24]

A distinction is made between "manifest," i.e., recognizable conflicts and "latent," i.e., hidden conflicts. The reference thereby is to conflicts assumed to be present, although they have (still) not become manifest.[25] If there are no conflicts which "can be directly pointed to," then signs are inventively discovered and interpreted as indicators that conflicts known to have occurred in the past are still going on, even if this is not readily apparent. Thus for example Geissler interprets phenomena such as "limited communication ability," "loss of motivation," "inability for interaction" or "professional fatigue" as "scars" through which the "central conflicts of our society become visible."[26]

Most authors assume that there will always be social conflicts: as soon as one is overcome, new ones arise.[27] Others affirm the possibility of a conflict-free society.[28] For so-called "late capitalistic society," to be sure, an "irreversible collapse of the system of legitimation" is asserted which makes probable an increase in the "conflict potential" of youth and "system critical behaviors and effects of the crisis of adolescence."[29]

Some authors assume or uncritically repeat that "conflict" is the basic category of the "political." According to Giesecke, the political is "what is disputed in society."[30] The conflict situation is "the actual political action situation."[31] It is conditioned by the fact of socio-economic inequality. "This inequality leads to conflicts which are the actual drive wheel of political processes and which are therefore the chief object of political engagement. Engagement in conflicts creates the possibility of reducing the level of inequality."[32]

Finally, in conflict pedagogics' image of man and society, conflict is held to provide an "especially knowledge-furthering learning situation." Conflict is claimed to increase motivation to learn, to further personality development, engagement, "ability to understand societal contradictions" and "competence for acting."[33]

Aims

What do the advocates of "conflict education" wish to achieve? There is agreement only on two points: first they want educands to acquire *knowledge* of social conflicts, their causes and effects as socio-cultural facts, as well as of the possibilities for the settlement and resolution of conflicts. We can call this aim "*ability to judge and resolve social conflicts.*"

Second, they desire that educands should acquire the readiness to "carry on,"[34] to "bear," to "deal with" or to "manage"[35] conflicts instead of "suppressing"[36] them and "adapting oneself at any price to the existing relationships."[37] We can refer to this aim as the "*readiness to bear and ability to manage social conflicts.*"[38] Some authors call this "readiness for conflict" or even "enthusiasm for conflict."[39] Theodor Ebert writes of "education for managing conflict."[40]

Opinions differ on what the "management" of conflict means, i.e., how educands ought to react to conflict. A rough distinction can be made among conflict-seeking, conflict-provoking, conflict-escalating, conflict-exploiting efforts, on the one side, and conflict-resolving, conflict-reducing, conflict-settling efforts, on the other. One can with Ebert distinguish between the "carrying on of conflict" and "conflict management."[41]

Authors with revolutionary intentions warn against so-called "technocratic conflict management," which "prevents existing dominance relationships from being encroached upon." They want to create "aggression potential" in educands which can be "employed against and for the elimination of the causes of frustration." Accordingly the call is made, under the name "critical peace pedagogics" or "aggression pedagogics," for "sharpening" conflicts. The aim in this case is the *ability to create, intensify and exploit conflict for political struggle* "toward a change in existing power constellations."[42]

The socialist author Johannes Beck advocates "education for *critique*, for *disobedience*, for *nonconformism*."[43] Individualistic left-liberals such as Giesecke want to achieve the following: "the *ability to engage oneself in manifest conflicts* for the sake of universal progress in democratization and *setting through one's own interests* and to bring this as much as possible to bear on latent conflicts."[44] As a single example of a "latent conflict" he refers to that between "capital and labor."[45]

Other authors are more inclined to emphasize skill in

"settling" conflicts. We can call this "*conflict settlement ability.*" It remains unclear, however, what sort of "settlement" is intended. While Oertel speaks vaguely of settlement "through individual" and "societal change,"[46] for Dencik, "conflict settlement" is the positive counter-concept to that of negatively valued "conflict suppression" through "appeasement strategies." In Dencik's opinion, conflict settlement ability includes "revolutionary strategy," whereby he understands "revolution" in the sense of a "necessary method to achieve a qualitative change in the established power structures." He regards "educational work"[47] to be part of this.

Schaller emphasizes that he is concerned with more than merely the "ability to live with conflict" and adjust to the prevailing situation. That would only be an "affirmation of the prevailing conflicts in existing reality." What should be achieved is rather the ability to "actively bring forth a new reality which transcends existing conflicts." Since he aims at an "improvement" of reality,[48] we can call his concept "*world improvement ability,*" or perhaps more cautiously "*desire for world improvement.*"

With each of these aim statements it remains unclear *which* societal conflicts are intended. We learn only that Giesecke is thinking of "the really fundamental, latent societal conflicts";[49] Lingelbach, of "the greater conflicts whose consequences affect the whole society,"[50] ones which are attributable to the "structural contradictions of the whole society";[51] and Oertel, of "age appropriate conflicts."[52]

It also deserves to be pointed out that I have never found reference in any texts to "conflict avoidance ability" as an aim of conflict education. This aim is currently not found in conflict pedagogics, but rather in popular self-improvement literature, e.g., in a book by Laura Huxley, which in German bears the old-fashioned title *Mastering Life: 33 Tested Methods for Living in Peace with your Friends and Neighbors.*[53]

Means

Instructing, explaining, transmitting information and argument are regarded as the chief means for the realization of the desired aims of conflict education.[54] In elevated pedagogical language, Schaller expounds on this: "Conflict education is carried out in the medium of rational argumentation," "in communicative interaction."[55] As means Giesecke names "conflict analysis" to be included in the "political instruction" of schools and in extra-curricular youth work.[56] He recommends that we elevate "conflict" to the "leading didactical principle."[57]

For Oertel, another educational means besides the treatment of social conflict in instruction is for "pedagogical specialists . . . at all levels of the educational and instructional system" to be "constantly ready to make the group's social behavior a matter of discussion and to let the current situation in the institution be questioned."[58] This means *instruction for constant moralizing reflexion and discussion of one's own group and the behavior of its members*—from kindergarten on up to the university and adult education.

Mollenhauer, to the contrary, regards as inadequate "explanation as a rational procedure occurring through the medium of the word" and considers as supplementary means the "educational arrangement of heterogeneous experiences" and "the *introduction of conflict situations*" into the life space and experiental worlds of educands.[59]

For the conflict education of "students and teachers with anti-capitalistic professional perspectives" Hans-G. Rolff and his co-workers have recommended *manoeuvers (planned games)* involving "*conflict simulation*," in which apparently "assertiveness skills" can be learned, "which they will need in their respective 'school struggle'."[60]

Ebert compiled a list of *conflict forms of non-violent action* which extends from protest demonstrations through legal non-cooperation to civil disobedience and civil usurpation.[61] He views forms of conflict as means "which should lead to attitudinal and behavioral changes, thus to learning processes"—for those who engage in them, for those against whom they act and for those who observe their employment.[62]

OUTLINES OF A CRITIQUE

I will first present a number of empirical viewpoints concerning factual questions, and thereafter certain normative viewpoints relating to valuative and normative issues.

Empirical Viewpoints

Education is always a means to an end.[63] This holds for actual educational actions, as well as for ones which are imagined, wished, proposed or called for. To scientifically test opinions about education or educational programs means to test what has been asserted about the relationships between ends and means in regard to specific educands in specific situations, and to attempt to determine whether these assertions are true. Or more cautiously expressed: whether they are sufficiently confirmed.[64] Every empirical test presupposes that such empirically testable factual assertions have already been formulated.

In our case of so-called "conflict pedagogics" this requirement has yet to be fulfilled. What we find is not an ordered system of testable empirical assertions, but merely a mishmash of vague, wishful notions.

1. The aims of conflict education are unclear. They are described in ambiguous and extremely vague terms. The term most often used, "conflict ability," is almost totally empty of substantive contents and can therefore be arbitrarily interpreted according to one's respective political, ideological, world-view and moral attitudes. Interpretations range from the "ability to evaluate conflicts" to "world improvement ability," from "conflict resolution ability" to "conflict incitation and escalation ability." An aim statement which refers to such variegated aims as ability to "theoretically analyze conflicts," "practically provoke conflicts," "resolve conflicts," "escalate conflicts" and "improve the world" is completely unusable as a starting point for a rational choice of means.

2. The aim statements of conflict education refer to ex-

tremely complex psychic dispositional networks which can probably only exist as intellectual constructs, but not as psychic reality. It is thereby not a matter of demonstrable (or realizable) psychic qualities, but rather of imagined qualities (hypothetical constructs) with limited empirical reference. Thus these aim concepts are theoretical concepts at the highest imaginable level of abstraction or generalization.

One can formulate useful aim statements only after the desired psychic dispositions are more precisely defined. This means that attributes must be added to general or genus concepts like "conflict ability" to create substantively richer and more narrowly demarcated (less extensive) concepts (species concepts). This would be necessary not only for the conceptual attribute "conflict," but also for that of "ability." As soon as that is attempted the following becomes apparent: conflict is not at all a genus concept under which "conflict of conscience," "marital disagreement," "civil disobedience," "general strike" or "war" can be classified as species concepts. Most of these have more in common with phenomena which are *not* called "conflict" than with ones which, because of a single attribute, such as "disagreement," "confrontation," or "dispute," can be classed as "conflicts." For scientific conflict research, which is oriented to precisely this unique phenomenon of "disagreement" in all its manifestations, this is perhaps no problem. If, however, not only real conflicts are studied, but a psychic disposition or personality quality called "conflict ability" is invented and passed off for an educational aim, problems arise which cannot be solved using the concept of conflict.

What is intended by so-called conflict education can probably only be clarified if the vague concepts of "conflict," "conflict ability," etc. are abandoned and clear conceptions arrived at through a differentiation and specification of the confused notions still associated with them. A variety of virtues will then be rediscovered which have long been known in both ethics and pedagogics, but have been temporarily forgotten in the enthusiasm for the study of conflicts.[65] Among them are not only virtues like wisdom, justness, courage, strength, readiness for national defense, self-discipline, patience, but also benevolence, trust, helpfulness, courtesy, peacefulness, selflessness, self-sufficiency, willingness for self-sacrifice, and sufferance.

3. In view of the vague, but at the same time extremely complex aim of "conflict ability," the statements made in so-called "conflict pedagogics" about the *means* through which this aim can presumably be realized appear "suspiciously simple and commonplace."[66] Only one thing is indisputable: *Knowledge* about conflicts and conflict settlement can be furthered through instruction; just so the ability to recognize, analyze and pass judgment on conflicts. But what should we make of such demanding aims as "conflict ability," "conflict settlement ability," "conflict avoidance ability" and the virtues meant thereby? It is unclear how the desired ends can be achieved using the recommended means.

Here again something has happened which often occurs in pedagogics: much more is promised by uncritical educational theoreticians than can be delivered. Authors are dissatisfied with what can be achieved through instruction in mass educational institutions, and accordingly set the highest and most comprehensive aims imaginable. The critique is thereby not "that pedagogues have great and noble aims, but rather that they make education—unexamined—the executor of these aims. They fail to ask: Is this eternal human ideal achievable? Achievable by me? Achievable through education? . . . Through means invented by me?"[67]

In my analysis of aims I have pointed out that the adherents of "conflict education" are insufficiently clear about what they want. Just for this reason they cannot name any proven, but at most supposed means. Therefore cliches and windy figures of speech run rampant like "rational argumentation," "communicative interaction," "regularly put up for discussion," "development of a critical action pattern in the conflictual surrounding."[68] It is claimed that "educational processes for coming to terms with conflict imply as societal analysis not only alternative critique, but also alternative public participation,"[69] etc. Scientific knowledge of appropriate means could only be acquired if *i.* the psychic dispositions aimed at by conflict education are empirically described and *ii.* the conditions for their creation under given life circumstances have been researched. Only when these conditions are known can it be determined whether aims are achievable and what means exist within the grasp of educators to create the necessary conditions.[70] It cannot be simpler.

4. Conflict pedagogical texts do not take into account the problem of *unwanted effects*. People and society, the world and life are one-sidedly represented from the viewpoint of conflict. If "conflict" is set as a "guiding didactic principle" and "conflict ability" as a central educational aim, then this is of necessity done at the cost of other principles and other educational aims, which thereby lose significance. Quite apart from the question of what is intended by "conflict ability," and whether it is achievable, even the propaganda of conflict pedagogics has effects for society and the individual. Above all, it is young, inexperienced persons who are prone to subjectively experience the world as others suggest they should. Whether the significance of conflict is emphasized or minimized by other people in the surrounding environment makes a great difference in a person's image of the world, general attitude, level of aspiration and attitude toward others. Undesired effects can thus result not only from the means but also from the proclaimed and realized aims of education. Those who fail to take these possibilities into account in their educational theories are empirically naive and act in a morally irresponsible manner.

Normative Viewpoints

"Conflict education" is only conceivable as a means to

ends. Ends are the starting point of every educational theory. They are known in educational science as educational aims, which can be viewed as norms indicating how educands ought to be and to what end their educators should educate them. A norm which calls for something to be brought about is called an "ideal."[71] A norm is only usable if it contains sufficient information about what is called for. We refer to this information as norm contents.

Educational aims like "conflict ability," "conflict management ability" or "conflict settlement ability" are personality ideals without statable norm contents. They are *normative empty formulas*.[72] Only because they lack specific contents are they accepted by the advocates of quite diverse world views and political aims. An empty formula looks like a generally accepted norm, but that is an illusion which quickly loses its plausibility when logically analyzed.

Norm contents, and thereby the usefulness of norms for the normative orientation of educands and educators, can only be agreed on in conflict education if we first decide on *which sorts* of conflicts we should take positions and also agree on the best *way* to do this. This will inevitably provoke differences of opinion. To resolve the latter it will then be necessary to develop a *value hierarchy* and define *norms with substantive norm contents*. Because they must be substantive, these norms will unavoidably be incompatible with the alternative substantive norms which could be realized in their place.

As long as one limits oneself to merely demanding that people should be ready and able to deal with conflicts, to end, master or resolve them, to manage or overcome them, everything remains shrouded in the fog of the non-obligatory. Decisive is *how* the demand is made to *evaluate* and *respond* to specific conflicts. This always depends on basic ideological-philosophical convictions, on views about right and wrong and the hierarchy of virtues. Differences in people's basic convictions inevitably cause them to perceive, classify and evaluate conflicts in different ways.

As soon as we focus on concrete conflicts, we also see clearly that conflict education is not merely a matter of conflicts as such, but rather is also concerned with the *objects* of conflicts. It is sensible to provide students with *knowledge* of conflicts, because one cannot judge conflicts without knowing the disputed objects and the aims and arguments of the disputants. However, *standards* are indispensable for *judgment,* and standards can differ greatly. In the case of education for conflict judgment ability it makes a profound difference whether the respectively possible standards for judgment are objectively presented and applied only in a comparative and provisional manner, or whether a single standard is one-sidedly set as absolute, as, for example, Giesecke does with his call for the pursuit of "personal interests," "equality" or "democratization."

Just as quite diverse standards exist for the judgment of conflict, there are a great variety of different attitudes, convictions and virtues that are promoted as psychic foundations for reacting to conflict. These range from the "readiness for class conflict" and for attempts to defeat the so-called "class enemy" to the Christian virtue of loving one's enemy; from the readiness to pursue "personal interests" to the readiness to subordinate them to the common good; from the readiness to hate enemies to the readiness to conciliate them.

Such various basic moral norms have nothing in common. Therefore it is misleading to hold to an empty formula like "conflict ability" or "disposition for conflict" which does not rule out any of these possible reactions to conflict. Anyone who means by "conflict education," "aggression education," "education for class conflict" or for the pursuit of "personal interests" should say so. Anyone who to the contrary means "education for peace," for love of peace, for conciliatory dispositions, for benevolence, for forgiving and fraternity should not be afraid to employ these clearer and more worthy names.

NOTES

1. To the best of my knowledge the German word "*Konfliktpädagogik*" was first employed by K. ROTH (1970) as a synonym for "Friedenspädagogik" (peace pedagogics). It is also employed by MANZ (1973: 110); MAIER (1973); K. GEISSLER (1977: 426); R. HERZOG (1978: 7); GIESECKE (1978: 498). BECK (1974: 148) speaks of "Pädagogik des Konflikts" (pedagogics of conflict), K. GEISSLER (1977: 434) *inter alia* of "konfliktorientierter Pädagogik" (conflict-oriented pedagogics). The related word "*Konfliktdidaktik*" (conflict didactics) is somewhat older and more common. It is found in, among others, HILLIGEN (1971: 83); LINGELBACH (1974); HORNUNG (1975: 30 ff.); UPLEGGER (1976); K. GEISSLER (1977); GIESECKE (1978: 500). MOLLENHAUER (1964: 110) appears to be the first to have written of the "pedagogical postulate" of "education for the management of conflict." On the history of the origins of "conflict didactics" and its sources in DAHRENDORF's conflict sociology (1959, 1961), cf. PFAUTZ (1974) (from the perspective of GDR pedagogics). Two recent articles on conflict and education in the USA: M. DEUTSCH (1993); JOHNSON and JOHNSON (1994).

2. *Oxford Latin Dictionary* (1968: 401 f.).

3. *Oxford English Dictionary*, 2nd ed. (1989, Vol. 3: 713).

4. Therefore R. HERZOG (1978: 7) errs in calling "so-called conflict pedagogics" a "branch of contemporary pedagogics."

5. Cf. WOLF (1970 and 1976); KISSLER (1977); OERTEL (1977).

6. WOLF (1970: 473 and 1976: 117).

7. Cf. MÖNNINGHOFF (1975); KROCKOW (1977).

8. Cf. MERTENS (1974); MOLLENHAUER (1972: 57) calls "conflict ability" an "aim dimension" which must be "postulated." On "conflict ability" as a "key qualification" cf. MÖNNINGHOFF (1975). ESSER (1977: 61) calls "the guiding aim of conflict ability a basis qualification."

9. SCHALLER (1970: 474).

10. GORDON (1970).

11. Brückner (1973: 179 and 12); cf. also (1970). On the world view of the New Left as fertile soil for these ideas cf. Brezinka (1981).

12. Dencik (1971: 268).

13. Dencik (1971: 264 f.).

14. Dencik (1971: 267 f.).

15. Dencik (1971: 256 f.). German: "Gewalt." This could also be translated as "force," "control," "power," "authority."

16. Lingelbach (1967: 53).

17. Mollenhauer (1968: 71).

18. Cf., e.g., N. Miller (1944); Lewin (1948); Murray (1968); Lückert (1957); Lehr (1965); Feger (1965 and 1972); M. Deutsch (1976).

19. Cf., e.g., Coser (1956, 1968); Krysmanski (1971).

20. Lückert (1964).

21. Dahrendorf (1961: 81).

22. In *Economy and Society* (1972: 20; 1978: 38 ff.) Weber employs the word "Kampf" (English: fight, struggle, combat, battle). The word "conflict" is used by the English translators: "A social relationship will be referred to as 'conflict' (Kampf) insofar as action is oriented intentionally to carrying out the actor's own will against the resistance of the other party or parties." Georg Simmel (1950, 1955, 1958) uses not only the term "Streit," but also "Kampf" and "Konflikt." Translations frequently obscure the terminological usage of German writers by employing "conflict" to render these words. Along with Marx, Weber and Simmel are considered as being among the most important "conflict" theorists.

23. Therefore as early as 1957 Bernard recommended avoiding the vague, ambiguous, emotionally and value-laden term "conflict," and replacing it with more precise, emotionally and value-neutral concepts. "It has no clear-cut referent. . . . It confuses analysis": (1957: 111).

24. Wolf (1970: 473).

25. Giesecke (1972: 143 and 162). As an example he names the "conflict between capital and labor." However, this is a basically non-visible "conflict" between two abstractions and does not fall under the concept of "social

conflict," but instead under that of "postulated conflict between hypothetical entities."

26. K. GEISSLER (1977: 431).

27. SCHALLER (1970: 474).

28. Thus, e.g., GIESECKE (1972: 143) argues that politically and societally "there must unavoidably be conflicts as a result of the historical process of democratization which has still not come to an end, and for this reason the formal opportunities for equality provided for in the German Constitution have in broad areas still not been realized for all." He thus seems to assume that upon the fulfillment of the conditions "democratization" and "equal opportunity," social conflicts will disappear or at least be greatly reduced.

29. DÖBERT and NUNNER-WINKLER (1973: 314 and 321).

30. GIESECKE (1969: 100).

31. GIESECKE (1972: 143). For a critique cf. NITSCH (1972).

32. GIESECKE (1972: 179).

33. KISSLER (1977: 181).

34. MOLLENHAUER (1964: 109); WOLF (1970: 473).

35. KISSLER (1977: 181); ESSER (1977: 58); a similar view: MOLLENHAUER (1964)

36. OERTEL (1977: 182).

37. WOLF (1970: 473).

38. E.g., NAHRSTEDT (1974: 142).

39. EBERT and JOCHHEIM (1970: 127).

40. ESSER (1977: 58).

41. EBERT and JOCHHEIM (1970: 128 ff.).

42. RAUCH and ANZINGER (1973: 126 f. and 339). More detailed on this DENCIK (1971).

43. BECK (1974: 148) (my italics).

44. GIESECKE (1972: 144) (my italics).

45. GIESECKE (1972: 143 and 162).

46. OERTEL (1977: 182).

47. DENCIK (1971: 249, 264, 267).

48. SCHALLER (1970: 474).

49. GIESECKE (1972: 145).

50. LINGELBACH (1967: 53).

51. LINGELBACH (1974: 343).

52. OERTEL (1977: 182).

53. HUXLEY (1972): *Das Leben meistern. 33 erprobte Methoden, mit dem lieben Nächsten in Frieden zu leben.* English: *You Are Not the Target* (1970).

54. Concrete working material for the conflict education of 8-13-year-old children from a Christian viewpoint is offered by DÖRING *et al.* (1975); methodical suggestions for work with secondary school pupils from a left-liberal viewpoint in ESSER (1977: 67 ff.).

55. SCHALLER (1970: 474).

56. GIESECKE (1972 and 1978: 500 f.).

57. GIESECKE (1978: 500).

58. OERTEL (1977: 182).

59. MOLLENHAUER (1968: 70 f.). For a justification cf. MOLLENHAUER (1964: 109): "The difficulty facing educational practice lies in that the traditional educational fields of family and school are relatively poor in conflicts."

60. ROLFF (1974: 264 ff.).

61. EBERT and JOCHHEIM (1970: 146 ff.).

62. EBERT and JOCHHEIM (1970: 131 ff.).

63. Cf. BREZINKA (1981: 106 ff.).

64. Cf. BREZINKA (1992: 53 ff.).

65. As an especially absurd example cf. the socialist psychoanalyst MENDEL (1973), who sets up *conflict "as a value in itself"* "under the conditions of the present," as *the* "new value" (p. 134), which together with "equality as a value" ought to take the place that in the condemned past was occupied by authority and obedience. He wishes the latter to be abolished in "a pedagogical revolution that will make the child equal to the adult" (p. 135).

66. BERNFELD (1928: 38).

67. BERNFELD (1928: 37).

68. K. GEISSLER (1977: 434).

69. ESSER (1977: 58).

70. Cf. BREZINKA (1992: 58 ff.) and in more detail (1981: 106 ff.).

71. Cf. BREZINKA (1994: 137 ff.).

72. Cf. TOPITSCH (1960). German: "Leerformel."

Bibliography

ACHINGER, GERTRUD and FELDMANN, KLAUS. 1971. 'Stellung und Funktion der Soziologie in der Lehrerbildung.' In: *Zeitschrift für Pädagogik*, 10th Supplement, pp. 135-139.

AEBLI, HANS. 1976. *Grundformen des Lehrens: eine allgemeine Didaktik auf kognitionspsychologischer Grundlage*, 9th ed. Stuttgart: Klett.

ALLERBECK, KLAUS R. and ROSENMAYR, LEOPOLD. 1976. *Einführung in die Jugendsoziologie*. Heidelberg: Quelle and Meyer.

ALLPORT, GORDON W. 1937. *Personality: A Psychological Interpretation*. New York: Henry Holt.

———. 1955. *Becoming: Basic Considerations for a Psychology of Personality*. New Haven, CT: Yale University Press.

———. 1962. 'Psychological Models for Guidance.' In: *Harvard Educational Review* 32, No. 4, pp. 373-381.

American Heritage Dictionary, Second College Edition. 1982. Boston: Houghton Mifflin.

ANDERSON, C. ARNOLD. 1964. 'Social.' In: JULIUS GOULD and WILLIAM L. KOLB (eds.). *A Dictionary of the Social Sciences*. New York: Free Press, p. 643.

APOSTEL, LEO. 1961. 'Towards the Formal Study of Models in the Non-formal Sciences.' In: HANS FREUDENTHAL (ed.). *The Concept and the Role of the Model in Mathematics and Natural and Social Sciences*. Dordrecht: Reidel, pp. 1-37.

168 Bibliography

ASCHERSLEBEN, KARL. 1983. *Didaktik*. Stuttgart: Kohlhammer.

———, and HOHMANN, MANFRED. 1979. *Handlexikon der Schulpädagogik*. Stuttgart: Kohlhammer.

AURIN, KURT (ed.). 1972. *Schulversuche in Planung und Erprobung. Innovationsstudien zur Schulreform an niedersächsischen Modellschulen und Schulversuchen*. Hannover: Schroedel.

AYTO, JOHN. 1990. *Bloomsbury Dictionary of Word Origins*. London: Bloomsbury.

BACH, HEINZ. 1975. 'Bedingungen der Sozialisation in der Schule.' In: *Überschaubare Schule*. Stuttgart: Klett, pp. 40-52.

BALDWIN, JAMES MARK (ed.). 1925. *Dictionary of Philosophy and Psychology*. New Edition. Reprinted 1960. Cloucester, MA: Smith.

BANDURA, ALBERT. 1971. *Psychological Modelling: Conflicting Theories*. New York: Atherton.

———, and WALTERS, RICHARD H. 1967. *Social Learning and Personality Development*. New York: Holt, Rinehart and Winston.

Barnhart Dictionary of Etymology. 1988. New York: H.W. Wilson.

BECK, JOHANNES. 1974. 'Konflikt. B. Der soziale Konflikt.' In: *Wörterbuch der pädagogischen Psychologie*. Freiburg: Herder, pp. 145-148.

BEKOFF, MARC. 1977. 'Socialization in Mammals with an Emphasis on Nonprimates.' In: SUZANNE CHEVALIER-SKOLNIKOFF and FRANK E. POIRIER (eds.). *Primate Bio-Social Development: Biological, Social, and Ecological Determinants*. New York: Garland, pp. 603-636.

BERGER, PETER L. and LUCKMANN, THOMAS. 1987. *The Social Construction of Reality. A Treatise in the Sociology of Knowledge*. New York: Penguin Books.

BERNARD, JESSIE. 1957. 'Parties and Issues in Conflict.' In: *The Journal of Conflict Resolution* 1, No. 2, pp. 111-121.

BERNFELD, SIEGFRIED. 1928. *Sisyphos oder die Grenzen der Erziehung*, 2nd ed. Vienna: Internationaler Psychoanalytischer Verlag.

BESTOR, ARTHUR E. 1948. 'The Evolution of the Socialist Vocabulary.' In: *Journal of the History of Ideas* IX, No. 3, pp. 259-302.

BITTNER, GÜNTHER. 1974. 'Sozialisation und Familie.' In: *Neue Sammlung* 14, pp. 324-326.

———. 1974a. 'Entwicklung' oder 'Sozialisation'?' In: *Neue Sammlung* 14, pp. 389-396.

BLANKERTZ, HERWIG. 1975. *Theorien und Modelle der Didaktik*, 9th ed. Munich: Juventa.

———. 1977. 'Die Verbindung von Abitur und Berufsausbildung. Konzept und Modellversuche zur Fortsetzung expansiver Bildungspolitik.' In: ANDREAS FLITNER and ULRICH HERRMANN (eds.). *Universität heute*. Munich: Piper, pp. 173-197.

BLASS, JOSEF LEONHARD. 1978. *Modelle pädagogischer Theorienbildung*, Vol. 2. Stuttgart: Kohlhammer.

BOMBACH, GOTTFRIED. 1965. 'Die Modellbildung in der Wirtschaftswissenschaft.' In: *Studium Generale* 18, pp. 339-346.

BRAITHWAITE, RICHARD B. 1962. 'Models in the Empirical Sciences.' In: ERNST NAGEL/PATRICK SUPPES/ALFRED TARSKI (eds.). *Logic, Methodology and Philosophy of Sciences*. Stanford, CA: Stanford University Press, pp. 224-231.

BREZINKA, WOLFGANG. 1981. *Erziehungsziele, Erziehungsmittel, Erziehungserfolg. Beiträge zu einem System der Erziehungswissenschaft*, 2nd ed. Munich: Reinhardt.

———. 1988. *Erziehung—Kunst des Möglichen. Beiträge zur Praktischen Pädagogik*, 3rd ed. Munich: Reinhardt.

———. 1992. *Philosophy of Educational Knowledge: An Introduction to the Foundations of the Science of Education, Philosophy of Education and Practical Pedagogics*. Dordrecht/Boston /London: Kluwer.

———. 1994. *Basic Concepts of Educational Science. Analysis, Critique, Proposals*. Lanham, MD/New York/London: University Press of America.

BRIM, ORVILLE G. 1966. 'Socialization Through the Life

Cycle.' In: ORVILLE G. BRIM and STANTON WHEELER. *Socialization after Childhood: Two Essays.* New York: John Wiley, pp. 1-49.

Brockhaus Enzyklopädie, 17th ed, Vol. 12. 1971. Wiesbaden: Brockhaus.

BRODBECK, MAY. 1968. 'Models, Meaning, and Theories.' In: MAY BRODBECK (ed.). *Readings in the Philosophy of the Social Sciences.* New York: Macmillan, pp. 579-600.

BRÜCKNER, PETER. 1970. 'Provokation als organisierte Selbstfreigabe.' In: HERMANN GIESECKE/DIETER BAACKE /HERMANN GLASER/THEODOR EBERT/GERNOT JOCHHEIM/ PETER BRÜCKNER. *Politische Aktion und politisches Lernen.* Munich: Juventa, pp. 175-235.

————. 1973. *Zur Sozialpsychologie des Kapitalismus.* 4th ed. Frankfurt: Europäische Verlagsanstalt.

BUBOLZ, GEORG (ed.). 1986. *Erziehungswissenschaftliches Lesebuch.* Frankfurt: Hirschgraben.

BÜLOW, FRIEDRICH. 1955. 'Sozial.' In: WILHELM BERNSDORF and FRIEDRICH BÜLOW (eds.). *Wörterbuch der Soziologie.* Stuttgart: Enke, pp. 465-466.

BUNDESMINISTER FÜR JUGEND, FAMILIE UND GESUNDHEIT. 1975. *Zweiter Familienbericht: Familie und Sozialisation.* Bonn.

BUNGE, MARIO. 1961. 'Kinds and Criteria of Scientific Laws.' In: *Philosophy of Science* 28, pp. 260-281.

————. 1973. *Method, Model and Matter.* Dordrecht: Reidel.

————. 1983. *Epistemologie: aktuelle Fragen der Wissenschaftstheorie.* Mannheim: Bibliographisches Institut.

BUSEMANN, ADOLF. 1935. 'Über Grundbegriffe der Kinder- und Jugendpsychologie.' In: *Acta psychologica* 1, pp. 49-64.

————. 1956. 'Ist die menschliche Jugend wirklich ein bloßer Entwicklungsprozeß?' In: LAURA DUPRAZ and EDUARD MONTALTA (eds.). *Die pädagogischen Gezeiten im Ablauf der menschlichen Jugend.* Fribourg, Switzerland: Universitätsverlag, pp. 25-39.

CARROLL, JOHN B. 1963. 'A Model of School Learning.' In: *Teachers College Record* 64, pp. 723-733.

CHAO, YUEN REN. 1962. 'Models in Linguistics and Models in General.' In: ERNEST NAGEL/PATRICK SUPPES/ALFRED TARSKI (eds.). *Logic, Methodology and Philosophy of Sciences.* Stanford, CA: Stanford University Press, pp. 558-566.

CHAPANIS, ALPHONSE. 1961. 'Men, Machines, and Models.' In: *American Psychologist* 16, No. 3, pp. 113-131.

CHEVALIER-SKOLNIKOFF, SUZANNE and POIRIER, FRANK E. (eds.). 1977. *Primate Bio-Social Development: Biological, Social, and Ecological Determinants.* New York: Garland.

CHILD, IRVIN L. 1954. 'Socialization.' In: GARDNER LINDZEY (ed.). *Handbook of Social Psychology, Vol. 2, Special Fields and Applications.* Reading, MA: Addison-Wesley, pp. 655-692.

————. 1972. 'Sozialisation (Sozialisierungsprozeß).' In: WILHELM BERNSDORF (ed.). *Wörterbuch der Soziologie.* Frankfurt: Fischer Taschenbuch, pp. 762-765.

CLAESSENS, DIETER. 1967. *Familie und Wertsystem. Eine Studie zur 'zweiten, sozio-kulturellen Geburt' des Menschen,* 2nd ed. Berlin: Duncker & Humblot.

CLAEYS, GREGORY. 1986. "Individualism,' 'Socialism,' and 'Social Science': Further Notes on a Process of Conceptual Formation, 1800-1850.' In: *Journal of the History of Ideas* 47, No. 1, pp. 81-93.

CLAUSEN, JOHN A. (ed.). 1968. *Socialization and Society.* Boston, MA: Little, Brown.

————. 1968a. 'Introduction.' In: JOHN A. CLAUSEN (ed.). *Socialization and Society.* Boston, MA: Little, Brown, pp. 1-17.

————. 1968b. 'A Historical and Comparative View of Socialization Theory and Research.' In: JOHN A. CLAUSEN (ed.). *Socialization and Society.* Boston, MA: Little, Brown, pp. 18-72.

CLAUSS, GÜNTER (ed.). 1976. *Wörterbuch der Psychologie.* Cologne: Pahl-Rugenstein.

COLLA, HERBERT E. 1981. *Heimerziehung. Stationäre Mo-*

172   Bibliography

delle und Alternativen. Munich: Kösel.

Collins German-English, English-German Dictionary. 1988. Glasgow: Collins.

COSER, LEWIS A. 1956. *The Functions of Social Conflict.* London: Free Press of Glencoe.

————. 1968. 'Conflict III. Social aspects.' In: DAVID L. SILLS (ed.). *International Encyclopedia of the Social Sciences,* Vol. 3. New York: Macmillan.

DAHRENDORF, RALF. 1959. *Class and Class Conflict in Industrial Society.* Stanford, CA: Stanford University Press.

————. 1961. *Gesellschaft und Freiheit.* Munich: Piper.

DEISSLER, HANS HERBERT/FRANK, KARL-OTTO/JAUSS, SOLVEIG /KERN, PETER CHR./KONIETZKO, CHRISTA/SAGI, ALEXANDER. 1978. *Der Freiburger Modellkindergarten. Konzeption, Erfahrungen, Anregungen.* Published by the Zentralverband katholischer Kindergärten und Kinderhorte Deutschlands e.V. Munich: Kösel.

DENCIK, LARS. 1971. 'Plädoyer für eine revolutionäre Konfliktforschung.' In: DIETER SENGHAAS (ed.). *Kritische Friedensforschung.* Frankfurt: Suhrkamp, pp. 247-270.

DEUTSCH, KARL W. 1963. *The Nerves of Government. Models of Political Communication and Control.* Glenco, IL: Free Press.

DEUTSCH, MORTON. 1973. *The Resolution of Conflict: Constructive and Destructive Processes.* New Haven, CT: Yale University Press.

————. 1993. 'Educating for a Peaceful World.' In: *American Psychologist* 48, No. 5, pp. 510-517.

DEWEY, JOHN. 1968. *Democracy and Education.* New York: Free Press.

DIECKMANN, JOHANN and BREITKREUZ, GERHARD. 1993. *Soziologie für Pädagogen.* Munich: R. Oldenbourg.

DIETRICH, THEO (ed.). 1969. *Unterrichtsbeispiele von Herbart bis zur Gegenwart,* 3rd ed. Bad Heilbrunn: Klinkhardt.

————, /ELZER, HANS-MICHAEL/FRANK, KARL-OTTO/MALSCH, OSKAR (eds.). 1972. *Schulpraktische Studien in der*

Lehrerbildung (= *Zeitschrift für Pädagogik*, 11th supplement). Weinheim: Beltz.

DÖBERT, RAINER and NUNNER-WINKLER, GERTRUD. 1973. 'Konflikt- und Rückzugspotentiale in spätkapitalistischen Gesellschaften.' In: *Zeitschrift für Soziologie* 2, pp. 301-325.

DOLCH, JOSEF. 1962. 'Einige Gedanken über Planung als Hilfe und Hemmung.' In: *Welt der Schule* 15, pp. 337-348.

——. 1965. *Grundbegriffe der pädagogischen Fachsprache*, 5th ed. Munich: Ehrenwirth.

DOLLARD, JOHN. 1939. 'Culture, Society, Impulse, and Socialization.' In: *American Journal of Sociology* 45, No. 1, pp. 50-63.

DÖRING, ULRIKE/BECKER, MANFRED/GROPP, STEPHAN/ GELLERT, MANFRED/HAUG, EGBERT/ HERMANN, URSULA/ HERMANNS, MARTIN/ HERZIG, WOLFGANG/ KUSENBERG, DORIS/ LISTEMANN, INGRID & HEINZ/ MATERN, WILHELM/MÜHLE, HEIDE/REICHLE, KARL/ WEISS, PETER. 1975. *Konflikte in der Kindergruppe. Arbeitsvorschläge zum Thema Konflikt und andere Anregungen zum Spielen, Erzählen, Gestalten.* Gelnhausen: Burckhardthaus.

DREVER, JAMES and FRÖHLICH, WERNER D. 1977. *dtv Wörterbuch zur Psychologie*, 10th ed. Munich: Deutscher Taschenbuch Verlag.

DUDEN. 1976-1981. *Das Große Wörterbuch der deutschen Sprache* in 6 Vols. Mannheim: Bibliographisches Institut.

——. 1989. *Etymologie. Herkunftswörterbuch der deutschen Sprache*. Mannheim: Dudenverlag.

——. 1989a. *Deutsches Universalwörterbuch*, 2nd ed. Mannheim: Dudenverlag.

DÜKER, HEINRICH and TAUSCH, REINHARD. 1957. 'Über die Wirkung der Veranschaulichung von Unterrichtsstoffen auf das Behalten.' In: *Zeitschrift für experimentelle und angewandte Psychologie* 4, pp. 384-400.

DURKHEIM, EMILE. 1956. *Education and Sociology*. Translated by SHERWOOD D. FOX. New York: Free Press.

174 Bibliography

————. 1961. *Moral Education: A Study in the Theory and Application of the Sociology of Education.* Translated by EVERETT K. WILSON and HERMAN SCHNURER. Glencoe: Free Press of Glencoe.

————. 1972. *Erziehung und Soziologie* (1922). Düsseldorf: Schwann.

————. 1973. *Erziehung, Moral und Gesellschaft.* Neuwied: Luchterhand.

EBERT, THEODOR and JOCHHEIM, GERNOT. 1970. 'Konfliktaustragung durch gewaltfreie Aktion.' In: HERMANN GIESECKE/DIETER BAACKE/HERMANN GLASER/ THEODOR EBERT/GERNOT JOCHHEIM/ PETER BRÜCKNER. *Politische Aktion und politisches Lernen.* Munich: Juventa, pp. 127-174.

EISLER, RUDOLF. 1929. *Wörterbuch der philosophischen Begriffe.* Berlin: Mittler.

ELKIN, FREDERICK. 1960. *The Child and Society. The Process of Socialization.* New York: Random House.

————, and HANDEL, GERALD. 1984. *The Child and Society. The Process of Socialization,* 4th ed. New York: Random House.

ESSER, JOHANNES. 1977. 'Curriculare Grundlagen einer schülerorientierten Konflikterziehung im Konfliktfeld Hauptschule.' In: GÜNTER BRINKMANN (ed.). *Praxis Hauptschule.* Kronberg: Scriptor, pp. 53-83.

EVERS, CARL-HEINZ. 1969. *Modelle moderner Bildungspolitik.* Frankfurt: Diesterweg.

FEGER, HUBERT. 1965. 'Beiträge zur experimentellen Analyse des Konflikts.' In: HANS THOMAE (ed.). *Allgemeine Psychologie. 2. Motivation (Handbuch der Psychologie,* Vol. 2). Göttingen: Hogrefe, pp. 332-412.

————. 1972. 'Gruppensolidarität und Konflikt.' In: CARL F. GRAUMANN (ed.). *Sozialpsychologie,* 2nd Half Vol. Göttingen: Hogrefe, pp. 1594-1653.

FEND, HELMUT. 1969. *Sozialisierung und Erziehung. Eine Einführung in die Sozialisierungsforschung.* Weinheim: Beltz.

————. 1971. 'Sozialisation (Sozialisierung).' In: *Lexikon*

der Pädagogik. New edition, Vol. 4. Freiburg: Herder, pp. 113-114.

————. 1971a. *Konformität und Selbstbestimmung. Mündigkeit und Leistungsmotivation in sozialisationstheoretischer Sicht.* Weinheim: Beltz.

————. 1974. *Gesellschaftliche Bedingungen schulischer Sozialisation.* Weinheim: Beltz.

FLITNER, ANDREAS. 1968. 'Modellschulen in Baden-Württemberg.' In: KULTUSMINISTERIUM BADEN-WÜRTTEMBERG (ed.). *Modellschulen in Baden-Württemberg.* Villingen: Neckar, pp. 3-21.

————. 1977. *Mißratener Fortschritt. Pädagogische Anmerkungen zur Bildungspolitik.* Munich: Piper.

FLITNER, WILHELM. 1954. *Grund- und Zeitfragen der Erziehung und Bildung.* Stuttgart: Klett.

————. 1954a. 'Der Ruf nach Modellschulen.' In: WILHELM FLITNER. *Grund- und Zeitfragen der Erziehung und Bildung.* Stuttgart: Klett, pp. 134-138.

————. 1956. 'Versuche, Modelle und Theorien in ihrer Bedeutung für die innere Schulreform.' In: *Die Deutsche Schule* 48, pp. 147-153.

FREUDENTHAL, HANS (ed.). 1961. *The Concept and the Role of the Model in Mathematics and Natural and Social Sciences.* Dordrecht: Reidel.

FREY, GERHARD. 1961. 'Symbolische und ikonische Modelle.' In: HANS FREUDENTHAL (ed.). *The Concept and the Role of the Model in Mathematics and Natural and Social Sciences.* Dordrecht: Reidel, pp. 89-97.

FREY, KARL (ed.). 1975. *Curriculum-Handbuch,* in 3 Vols. Munich: Piper.

FRISBY, DAVID. 1992. *Simmel and Since. Essays on Georg Simmel's Social Theory.* London: Routledge.

FRÖHLICH, WERNER D. and WELLEK, STEFAN. 1972. 'Der begrifflich-theoretische Hintergrund der Sozialisationsforschung.' In: CARL F. GRAUMANN (ed.). *Sozialpsychologie,* 2nd Half Vol. Göttingen: Hogrefe, pp. 661-714.

GECK, LUDWIG HEINRICH ADOLPH. 1963. *Über das Eindringen des Wortes 'sozial' in die deutsche Sprache.*

Göttingen: Schwartz.

GEHLEN, ARNOLD. 1988. *Man: His Nature and Place in the World*. Translated by CLARE MCMILLAR and KARL PILLEMER. New York: Columbia University Press.

GEISSLER, HARALD. 1977. *Modelle der Unterrichtsmethode*. Stuttgart: Klett-Cotta.

GEISSLER, KARLHEINZ A. 1977. 'Die pädagogische Relevanz von Konflikten.' In: *Die Deutsche Schule* 69, pp. 426-435.

GEORGES, KARL ERNST. 1962. *Ausführliches lateinisch-deutsches Handwörterbuch*, 11th ed. Hannover: Hahn.

GEULEN, DIETER. 1973. 'Thesen zur Metatheorie der Sozialisation.' In: HEINZ WALTER (ed.). *Sozialisationsforschung*, Vol. 1. Stuttgart: Frommann, pp. 85-101.

———. 1977. *Das vergesellschaftete Subjekt. Zur Grundlegung der Sozialisationstheorie*. Frankfurt: Suhrkamp.

———. 1980. 'Die historische Entwicklung sozialisationstheoretischer Paradigmen.' In: KLAUS HURRELMANN and DIETER ULICH (eds.). *Handbuch der Sozialisationsforschung*. Weinheim: Beltz, pp. 15-49.

———. 1991. 'Die historische Entwicklung sozialisationstheoretischer Ansätze.' In: KLAUS HURRELMANN and DIETER ULICH (eds.). *Neues Handbuch der Sozialisationsforschung*, 4th revised ed. Weinheim: Beltz, pp. 21-54.

———, and HURRELMANN, KLAUS. 1980. 'Zur Programmatik einer umfassenden Sozialisationstheorie.' In: KLAUS HURRELMANN and DIETER ULICH (eds.). *Handbuch der Sozialisationsforschung*. Weinheim: Beltz, pp. 51-67.

GIDDINGS, FRANKLIN HENRY. 1897. *The Theory of Socialization: A Syllabus of Sociological Principles*. New York/London: Macmillan.

GIESECKE, HERMANN. 1969. *Didaktik der politischen Bildung*, 4th ed. Munich: Juventa.

———. 1972. *Didaktik der politischen Bildung. Neue Ausgabe*. Munich: Juventa.

———. 1978. 'Konflikt.' In: HELMWART HIERDEIS (ed.). *Taschenbuch der Pädagogik*. Baltmannsweiler: Schneider, pp. 497-503.

———. 1985. *Das Ende der Erziehung*. Stuttgart: Klett-Cotta.

———, BAACKE, DIETER/GLASER, HERMANN/EBERT, THEODOR /JOCHHEIM, GERNOT/ BRÜCKNER, PETER. 1970. *Politische Aktion und politisches Lernen*. Munich: Juventa.

GILGENMANN, KLAUS. 1986. 'Autopoiesis und Selbstsozialisation.' In: *Zeitschrift für Sozialisationsforschung und Erziehungssoziologie* 6, pp. 71-90.

GLÄSS, THEO and KLAFKI, WOLFGANG. 1961. 'Schulversuche und Versuchsschulen.' In: *Pädagogisches Lexikon*. Stuttgart: Kreuz, cols. 872-875.

GLOGAUER, WERNER. 1967. *Das Strukturmodell der Didaktik*. Munich: Ehrenwirth.

GORDON, THOMAS. 1970. *Parent Effectiveness Training. The 'No-Lose' Program for Raising Responsible Children*. New York: Peter H. Wyden.

GOSLIN, DAVID A. (ed.). 1969. *Handbook of Socialization Theory and Research*. Chicago: Rand McNally.

———. 1971. 'Socialization.' In: LEE C. DEIGHTON (ed.). *Encyclopedia of Education*. New York: Macmillan and Free Press, Vol. 8., pp. 300-308.

GRIMM, JACOB and GRIMM, WILHELM. 1962. *Deutsches Wörterbuch*, Vol. 6. Leipzig: Hirzel.

GRUHL, HEIDI M. 1983. *Sozialisation als kategorische Erfassung von Welt*. Philosophische Dissertation. Bonn.

GUKENBIEHL, HERMANN L. 1973. 'Sozialisation als gesellschaftsbedingter und gesellschaftsrelevanter Prozeß.' In: INGRID GIRSCHNER-WOLDT/GUKENBIEHL, HERMANN L./SCHÄFERS, BERNHARD/ WÖHLER, KARL-HEINZ. *Soziologie für Pädagogen. Beiträge zum erziehungswissenschaftlichen Studium*. Stuttgart: Enke, pp. 39-84.

HABERMAS, JÜRGEN. 1973. 'Stichworte zur Theorie der Sozialisation.' In: *Kultur und Kritik*. Frankfurt: Suhrkamp, pp. 118-194.

HAIN, ULRICH and RICKER, GÜNTHER (eds.). 1980. *Das Gie-ßener didaktische Modell.* Frankfurt: Fachbuch-handlung für Psychologie.

HALBFAS, HUBERTUS/MAURER, FRIEDEMANN/POPP, WALTER (eds.). 1976. *In Modellen denken.* Stuttgart: Klett.

HARTMANN, NICOLAI. 1966. *Teleologisches Denken,* 2nd ed. Berlin: De Gruyter.

HARTMANN, PETER. 1965. 'Modellbildungen in der Sprach-wissenschaften.' In: *Studium Generale* 18, pp. 364-379.

HASSENSTEIN, BERNHARD. 1973. *Verhaltensbiologie des Kindes.* Munich: Piper.

――――. 1974. 'Das Projekt 'Tagesmütter.'' In: *Zeitschrift für Pädagogik* 20, pp. 415-426.

HEGEL, FRIEDRICH. 1970. *Enzyklopädie der philosophi-schen Wissenschaften im Grundrisse* (1830). In: *Werke,* Vol. 10. Frankfurt: Suhrkamp.

HEHLMANN, WILHELM. 1971. *Wörterbuch der Pädagogik,* 10th ed. Stuttgart: Kröner.

HEINZ, WALTER R. 1976. 'Sozialisation.' In: LEO ROTH (ed.). *Handlexikon zur Erziehungswissenschaft.* Mu-nich: Ehrenwirth, pp. 412-417.

HENTIG, HARTMUT VON. 1964. 'Planung entwickelt eine neue Mentalität.' In: ROBERT JUNGK and HANS JOSEF MUNDT (eds.). *Modell für eine neue Welt: Der Griff nach der Zukunft.* Munich: Desch, pp. 157-180.

――――. 1965. *Die Schule im Regelkreis. Ein neues Modell für die Probleme der Erziehung und Bildung.* Stuttgart: Klett.

――――. 1966. *Analysen und Modelle zur Schulreform. Drit-tes Sonderheft der Neuen Sammlung.* Göttingen: Vandenhoeck & Ruprecht.

――――. 1968. *Systemzwang und Selbstbestimmung. Über die Bedingungen der Gesamtschule in der Indu-striegesellschaft.* Stuttgart: Klett.

HERBART, JOHANN FRIEDRICH. 1913/19. *Pädagogische Schriften,* 3rd ed. Edited by OTTO WILLMANN and THEODOR FRITZSCH. Osterwieck: Zickfeldt.

――――. 1977. *Outlines of Educational Doctrine* (1911). Translated by ALEXIS F. LANGE. New York/London:

Macmillan. Reprinted *sine loco*: Folcroft Library Editions.

HERRMANN, ULRICH. 1987. 'Familie, Kindheit, Jugend.' In: KARL-ERNST JEISMANN and PETER LUNDGREEN (eds.). *Handbuch der deutschen Bildungsgeschichte*, Vol. 3. *1800-1870: Von der Neuordnung Deutschlands bis zur Gründung des Deutschen Reiches*. Munich: Beck, pp. 53-69.

HERZOG, ROMAN. 1978. 'Erziehung ohne Inhalt? Um die Prinzipien der Bildungsreform.' In: *Die Politische Meinung* 23, No. 178, pp. 5-10.

HESS, ECKARD H. 1975. *Prägung. Die frühkindliche Entwicklung von Verhaltensmustern bei Tier und Mensch*. Munich: Kindler.

HESSE, MARY B. 1966. *Models and Analogies in Science*. Notre Dame, IN: University of Notre Dame Press.

———. 1967. 'Models and Analogy in Science.' In: PAUL EDWARDS (ed.). *The Encyclopedia of Philosophy*, Vol. 5. New York: Macmillan, pp. 354-359.

HEUMANN, HANS. 1966. 'Lehrmittel und Lehrmittelsammlungen.' In: WALTER HORNEY/JOHANN PETER RUPPERT/WALTER SCHULTZE/HANS SCHEUERL (eds.). *Handbuch für Lehrer*, Vol. 1. Gütersloh: Bertelsmann, pp. 341-354.

HILKER, FRANZ. 1924. 'Versuchsschulen und allgemeine Schulreform.' In: FRANZ HILKER (ed.). *Deutsche Schulversuche*. Berlin: Schwetschke, pp. 448-463.

HILLER, GOTTHILF G. 1971. 'Unterrichtsmodelle, Unterrichtskonstruktion.' In: *Lexikon der Pädagogik*, Vol. 4. Freiburg: Herder, p. 275.

———. 1973. *Konstruktive Didaktik. Beiträge zur Definition von Unterrichtszielen durch Lehrformen und Unterrichtsmodelle*. Düsseldorf: Schwann.

———. 1976. 'Alltägliche Modellvorstellungen und didaktische Rekonstruktionen.' In: HUBERTUS HALBFAS/FRIEDEMANN MAURER/WALTER POPP (eds.). *In Modellen denken*. Stuttgart: Klett, pp. 144-169.

HILLIGEN, WOLFGANG. 1971. 'Zu einer Didaktik des Konflikts.' In: *Gesellschaft, Staat, Erziehung* 16, pp. 82-93.

180   Bibliography

HORNUNG, KLAUS. 1975. 'Zwischen offener Gesellschaft
    und ideologischem Dogmatismus. 30 Jahre politi-
    sche Bildung und Erziehung in der Bundesrepub-
    lik.' In: PETER GUTJAHR-LÖSER and HANS-HELMUTH
    KNÜTTER (eds.). Der Streit um die politische Bil-
    dung. Munich: Olzog, pp. 15-42.
HURRELMANN, KLAUS. 1975. Erziehungssystem und Gesell-
    schaft. Reinbek: Rowohlt.
————. (ed.) 1976. Sozialisation und Lebenslauf: Empirie
    und Methodik sozialwissenschaftlicher Persönlich-
    keitsforschung. Reinbek: Rowohlt.
————. 1977. 'Sozialisation in soziologischer Sicht.' In:
    Wörterbuch der Pädagogik, Vol. 3. Freiburg: Her-
    der, pp. 175-177.
————, and ULICH, DIETER (eds.). 1980. Handbuch der
    Sozialisationsforschung. Weinheim: Beltz.
————, and ULICH, DIETER (eds.). 1991. Neues Handbuch
    der Sozialisationsforschung, 4th revised ed. Wein-
    heim: Beltz.
HUXLEY, LAURA ARCHERA. 1970. You Are Not the Target.
    With a foreword by ALDOUS HUXLEY. North Holly-
    wood, CA: Wilshire.
————. 1972. Das Leben meistern. 33 erprobte Methoden,
    mit dem lieben Nächsten in Frieden zu leben.
    Hamburg: Schröder.
IBEN, GERD. 1975. "Abweichende' and 'defizitäre' Soziali-
    sation.' In: FRIEDHELM NEIDHARDT (ed.). Frühkind-
    liche Sozialisation. Stuttgart: Enke, pp. 114-161.
INKELES, ALEX. 1966. 'Social Structure and the Socializa-
    tion of Competence.' In: Harvard Educational Re-
    view 36, pp. 265-283.
————. 1968. 'Society, Social Structure, and Child Social-
    ization.' In: JOHN A. CLAUSEN (ed.). Socialization
    and Society. Boston, MA: Little, Brown, pp. 73-
    129.
————. 1969. 'Social Structure and Socialization.' In:
    DAVID A. GOSLIN (ed.). Handbook of Socialization
    Theory and Research. Chicago: Rand McNally, pp.
    615-632.
JACOBSON, MILTON D./STIMART, REYNOLD P./WREN, GEORGE

T. 1971. 'Models and Educational Research.' In: *American Educational Research Journal* 8, No. 2, pp. 311-320.

JAMMER, MAX. 1965. 'Die Entwicklung des Modellbegriffes in den physikalischen Wissenschaften.' In: *Studium Generale* 18, pp. 166-173.

JOHNSON, DAVID W. and JOHNSON, ROGER T. 1994. 'Constructive Conflict in the Schools.' In: *Journal of Social Issues* 50, No. 1, pp. 117-137.

KAHN, HERMAN. 1977. *Vor uns die guten Jahre. Ein realistisches Modell unserer Zukunft.* Vienna: Molden.

KAINZ, FRIEDRICH. 1962. *Psychologie der Sprache*, Vol. 1, 3rd ed. Stuttgart: Enke.

———. 1972. *Über die Sprachverführung des Denkens.* Berlin: Duncker & Humblot.

KANT, IMMANUEL. 1963. *Ausgewählte Schriften zur Pädagogik und ihrer Begründung.* Edited by HANS-HERMANN GROOTHOFF. Paderborn: Schöningh.

KAPLAN, ABRAHAM. 1964. *The Conduct of Inquiry. Methodology for Behavioral Science.* San Francisco: Chandler.

KARRENBERG, FRIEDRICH. 1965. 'Sozialisierung.' In: *Evangelisches Soziallexikon.* Stuttgart: Kreuz, cols. 1136-1137.

KERSTIENS, LUDWIG. 1974. *Modelle emanzipatorischer Erziehung. Eine Zwischenbilanz. Voraussetzungen—Entwürfe—Kritik.* Bad Heilbrunn: Klinkhardt.

KEUCHEL, HERMANN. 1983. 'Das 'Modell' Aachen. Entstehung und Verwirklichung.' In: DER BUNDESMINISTER FÜR BILDUNG UND WISSENSCHAFT: *Informationen Bildung/Wissenschaft*, No. 5/83 (26 May), pp. 82-85.

KISSLER, LEO. 1977. 'Konflikt, Konflikterziehung.' In: *Wörterbuch der Pädagogik*, Vol. 2. Freiburg: Herder, pp. 180-181.

KLAUS, GEORG and BUHR, MANFRED (eds.). 1975. *Philosophisches Wörterbuch*, 11th ed. Berlin: das europäische Buch.

KLAUSMEIER, HERBERT and RIPPLE, RICHARD E. 1973. *Moderne Unterrichtspsychologie*, Vol. 1. Munich:

Reinhardt.

———. 1975. *Moderne Unterrichtspsychologie*, Vol. 3. Munich: Reinhardt.

KLOTZ, GÜNTER R. 1975. 'Modelle der Zusammenarbeit mit der Bildungsindustrie.' In: KARL FREY (ed.). *Curriculum-Handbuch*, in 3 Vols. Munich: Piper, Vol. 3, pp. 142-148.

KLOTZ, REINHOLD (ed.). 1963. *Handwörterbuch der lateinischen Sprache*, 7th ed. Graz, AU: Akademische Druckanstalt.

KNOLL, JÖRG. 1978. 'Sozialisation und Erziehung.' In: HELMWART HIERDEIS (ed.). *Taschenbuch der Pädagogik*. Baltmannsweiler: Schneider, pp. 727-740.

KNOSPE, HORST. 1972. 'Sozial, das Soziale.' In: WILHELM BERNSDORF (ed.). *Wörterbuch der Soziologie*. Frankfurt: Fischer, pp. 708-710.

KOB, JANPETER. 1976. *Soziologische Theorie der Erziehung*. Stuttgart: Kohlhammer.

KONDAKOW, NIKOLAJ I. 1978. *Wörterbuch der Logik*. Berlin: Verlag das europäische Buch.

KÖNIG, ECKARD. 1980. 'Legitimationsprobleme didaktischer Modelle.' In: ULRICH HAIN and GÜNTHER RICKER (eds.). *Das Gießener didaktische Modell*. Frankfurt: Fachbuchhandlung für Psychologie, pp. 39-44.

KÖNIG, RENE. 1955. 'Soziologie der Familie.' In: ARNOLD GEHLEN and HELMUT SCHELSKY (eds.). *Soziologie*. Düsseldorf: Diederichs, pp. 121-158.

———. 1974. *Materialien zur Soziologie der Familie*, 2nd ed. Cologne: Kiepenheuer und Witsch.

KRAMPEN, GÜNTER and BRANDSTÄDTER, JOCHEN. 1981. 'Kognitionspsychologische Analysen erzieherischen Handelns: Instrumentalitätstheoretische Ansätze.' In: MANFRED HOFER (ed.). *Informationsverarbeitung und Entscheidungsverhalten von Lehrern. Beiträge zu einer Handlungstheorie des Unterrichtens*. Munich: Urban & Schwarzenberg, pp. 222-254.

KRECH, DAVID and KLEIN, GEORGE S. (eds.). 1952. *Theoretical Models and Personality Theory*. Durham, NC: Duke University Press.

KREUZER, KARL JOSEF. 1978. Das Modellprojekt "Tagesmütter." In: RAINER DOLLASE (ed.). *Handbuch der Früh- und Vorschulpädagogik.* Düsseldorf: Schwann, pp. 171-176.

KRIECK, ERNST. 1922. *Philosophie der Erziehung.* Jena: Diederichs.

———. 1933. *Menschenformung. Grundzüge der vergleichenden Erziehungswissenschaft,* 2nd ed. Leipzig: Quelle & Meyer.

———. 1934. *Grundlegende Erziehung,* 3rd ed. Erfurt: Stenger.

KROCKOW, CHRISTIAN VON. 1977. 'Konfliktfähigkeit. Grundbedingung der demokratischen Gesellschaft.' In: *Vorgänge* 16, No. 30, pp. 13-19.

KRYSMANSKI, HANS-JÜRGEN. 1971. *Soziologie des Konflikts.* Reinbek: Rowohlt.

KUCKARTZ, WILFRIED. 1969. *Sozialisation und Erziehung. Eine Polemik wider den Pädagogismus.* Essen: Neue Deutsche Schule.

KUHN, THOMAS S. 1970. *The Structure of Scientific Revolutions,* 2nd ed. Chicago: University of Chicago Press.

KULTUSMINISTERIUM BADEN-WÜRTTEMBERG (ed.). 1968. *Modellschulen in Baden-Württemberg.* Villingen: Neckar.

LACEY, COLIN. 1985. 'Professional Socialization of Teachers.' In: TORSTEN HUSEN and T. NEVILLE POSTLETHWAITE (eds.). *International Encyclopedia of Education. Research and Studies.* Oxford: Pergamon, Vol. 7, pp. 4073-4084.

LEHMANN, RAINER. 1977. *Modell und Methoden in der empirischen Erziehungsforschung.* Munich: Ehrenwirth.

LEHR, URSULA. 1965. *Erscheinungsweisen des Konflikts.* In: HANS THOMAE (ed.). *Allgemeine Psychologie. 2. Motivation (Handbuch der Psychologie,* Vol. 2). Göttingen: Hogrefe, pp. 306-331.

LEWIN, KURT. 1948. *Resolving Social Conflicts. Selected Papers on Group Dynamics.* Edited by GERTRUD WEISS LEWIN. New York: Harper.

LINGELBACH, KARL C. 1967. 'Der 'Konflikt' als Grundbegriff der Politischen Bildung.' In: *Pädagogische Rundschau* 21, pp. 48-55 and 125-138.

———. 1974. 'Konflikt.' In: CHRISTOPH WULF (ed.). *Wörterbuch der Erziehung*. Munich: Piper, pp. 337-347.

LIPPITT, RONALD. 1968. 'Improving the Socialization Process.' In: JOHN A. CLAUSEN (ed.). *Socialization and Society*. Boston, MA: Little, Brown, pp. 321-374.

LOCH, WERNER (ed.). 1978. *Modelle pädagogischen Verstehens*. Essen: Neue Deutsche Schule.

LOCHNER, RUDOLF. 1975. *Phänomene der Erziehung. Erscheinungsweisen und Ablaufformen im personalen und ethnischen Dasein*. Meisenheim: Hain.

———. 1976. 'Über das Grundverhältnis zwischen Anthropologie und Erziehungswissenschaft' (1952). In: DIETER HÖLTERSHINKEN (ed.). *Das Problem der Pädagogischen Anthropologie im deutschsprachigen Raum*. Darmstadt: Wissenschaftliche Buchgesellschaft, pp. 127-142.

LONG, THEODORE E. and HADDEN, JEFFREY K. 1985. 'A Reconception of Socialization.' In: *Sociological Theory* 3, No. 1, pp. 39-49.

Longman Dictionary of Contemporary English, New Edition. 1987. New York: Longman.

LÜCKERT, HEINZ-ROLF. 1957. *Konfliktpsychologie*, 6th ed. Munich: Reinhardt.

———. 1964. *Der Mensch—das konfliktträchtige Wesen*. Munich: Reinhardt.

LÜSCHER, KURT. 1977. 'Sozialpolitik für das Kind.' In: CHRISTIAN VON FERBER (ed.). *Soziologie und Sozialpolitik. Sonderheft der Kölner Zeitschrift für Soziologie und Sozialpsychologie*, No. 19, pp. 591-628.

MACHWIRTH, ECKART. 1974. 'Sozialisation.' In: HEINZ-JÜRGEN IPFLING (ed.). *Grundbegriffe der pädagogischen Fachsprache*. Munich: Ehrenwirth, pp. 263-266.

MADER, OSKAR. 1979. *Fragen der Lehrplantheorie*. Berlin: Volk und Wissen.

MAGDEBURG, HORST. 1967. *Gesamtschule. Modell für die Schule von morgen?* Weinheim: Beltz.

MAIER, HANS. 1973. 'Grenzen der Konfliktpädagogik.' In: *Politische Bildung* 6, No. 4, pp. 65-68.

MANZ, WOLFGANG. 1973. 'Konflikt.' In: GERHARD WEHLE (ed.). *Pädagogik aktuell. Lexikon pädagogischer Schlagworte und Begriffe*, Vol. 1. Munich: Kösel, pp. 109-110.

MARTINAK, EDUARD. 1908. 'Präparieren.' In: JOSEPH LOOS (ed.). *Enzyklopädisches Handbuch der Erziehungskunde*, in 2 Vols. Vienna: Pichler, Vol. 2, pp. 321-327.

MÄRZ, FRITZ. 1978. *Problemgeschichte der Pädagogik, Vol. 1: Die Lern- und Erziehungsbedürftigkeit des Menschen*. Bad Heilbrunn: Klinkhardt.

MASTERMAN, MARGARET. 1970. 'The Nature of a Paradigm.' In: IMRE LAKATOS and ALAN MUSGRAVE (eds.). *Criticism and the Growth of Knowledge*. Cambridge: Cambridge University Press, pp. 59-89.

MAYER, RICHARD E. 1989. 'Models for Understanding.' In: *Review of Educational Research* 59, No. 1, pp. 43-64.

MAYNTZ, RENATE (ed.). 1967. *Formalisierte Modelle in der Soziologie*. Neuwied: Luchterhand.

McDOUGALL, WILLIAM. 1908. *An Introduction to Social Psychology*. 1963 reprint. London: Methuen.

MEISTER, RICHARD. 1947. *Beiträge zur Theorie der Erziehung*, 2nd ed. Vienna: Sexl.

MEMMERT, WOLFGANG. 1977. *Didaktik in Grafiken und Tabellen*. Bad Heilbrunn: Klinkhardt.

MENDEL, GERARD. 1973. *Plädoyer für die Entkolonisierung des Kindes. Soziopsychoanalyse der Autorität*. Olten: Walter.

MERTENS, WOLFGANG. 1974. *Erziehung zur Konfliktfähigkeit. Vernachlässigte Dimensionen der Sozialisationsforschung*. Munich: Ehrenwirth.

METZGER, WOLFGANG. 1965. 'Über Modellvorstellungen in der Psychologie.' In: *Studium Generale* 18, pp. 346-352.

Meyers Enzklopädisches Lexikon, 9th ed., Vol. 16. 1976. Mannheim: Bibliographisches Institut.

MILLER, NEAL E. 1944. 'Experimental Studies of Conflict.'

186 Bibliography

In: JOSEPH MCVICKER HUNT (ed.). *Personality and the Behavior Disorders.* Vol. 1. New York: Ronald, pp. 431-465.

MOLLENHAUER, KLAUS. 1964. 'Gesellschaft in pädagogischer Sicht.' In: HANS-HERMANN GROOTHOFF (ed.). *Pädagogik.* Frankfurt: Fischer Lexikon, pp. 102-112.

————. 1968. *Erziehung und Emanzipation.* Munich: Juventa.

————. 1969. 'Sozialisation und Schulerfolg.' In: HEINRICH ROTH (ed.) *Begabung und Lernen. Ergebnisse und Folgerungen neuer Forschungen.* Stuttgart: Klett, pp. 269-296.

————. 1971. 'Sozialisation.' In: *Neues Pädagogisches Lexikon.* Stuttgart: Kreuz, cols. 1068-1073.

————. 1972. *Theorien zum Erziehungsprozeß.* Munich: Juventa.

MÖLLER, BERNHARD. 1966. *Analytische Unterrichtsmodelle. Ergebnisse und Probleme der wissenschaftlichen Lernorganisation.* Munich: Reinhardt.

MÖNNINGHOFF, JÖRG. 1975. 'Lernziel Konfliktfähigkeit.' In: *Deutsche Jugend* 23, pp. 31-39.

MONTADA, LEO. 1982. 'Themen, Traditionen, Trends.' In: ROLF OERTER and LEO MONTADA (eds.). *Entwicklungspsychologie.* Munich: Urban & Schwarzenberg, pp. 3-88.

MÜHLBAUER, KARL REINHOLD. 1980. *Sozialisation: Eine Einführung in Theorien und Modelle.* Munich: Wilhelm Fink.

————. 1986. 'Sozialisation.' In: ERICH WASEM (ed.). *Studienfach Pädagogik.* Baltmannsweiler: Schneider, pp. 180-195.

MÜHLE, GÜNTHER. 1969. 'Definitions- und Methodenprobleme der Begabungsforschung.' In: HEINRICH ROTH (ed.). *Begabung und Lernen. Ergebnisse und Folgerungen neuer Forschungen.* Stuttgart: Klett, pp. 69-97.

————. 1972. 'Entwicklung.' In: JOACHIM RITTER (ed.). *Historisches Wörterbuch der Philosophie,* Vol. 2. Basel: Schwabe, pp. 557-560.

MÜLLER, GERT H. 1965. 'Der Modellbegriff in der Mathematik.' In: *Studium Generale* 18, pp. 154-166.

MÜLLER, HANS. 1967. *Ursprung und Geschichte des Wortes 'Sozialismus' und seiner Verwandten.* Hannover: J.H.W. Dietz.

MÜLLER, ROLAND. 1980. 'Zur Geschichte des Modellbegriffs und des Modelldenkens im Bezugsfeld der Pädagogik.' In: HERBERT STACHOWIAK (ed.). *Modelle und Modelldenken im Unterricht. Anwendung der allgemeinen Modelltheorie auf die Unterrichtspraxis.* Bad Heilbrunn: Klinkhardt, pp. 202-224.

MÜNDER, JOHANNES. 1985. *Familien- und Jugendrecht. Eine sozialwissenschaftlich orientierte Darstellung des Rechts der Sozialisation,* 2nd ed. Weinheim: Beltz.

MURRAY, EDWARD J. 1968. 'Conflict. I. Psychological Aspects.' In: DAVID L. SILLS (ed.). *International Encyclopedia of the Social Sciences.* New York: Macmillan, Vol. 3, pp. 220-226.

NAGEL, ERNEST. 1961. *The Structure of Science: Problems in the Logic of Scientific Explanation.* New York: Harcourt, Brace & World.

————, /SUPPES, PATRICK/TARSKI, ALFRED (eds.). 1962. *Logic, Methodology and Philosophy of Sciences.* Stanford, CA: Stanford University Press.

NAHRSTEDT, WOLFGANG. 1974. *Freizeitpädagogik in der nachindustriellen Gesellschaft,* Vol. 1. Neuwied: Luchterhand.

NEIDHARDT, FRIEDHELM. 1970. 'Sozialisation.' In: WALTER HORNEY/JOHANN PETER RUPPERT/WALTER SCHULTZE /HANS SCHEUERL (eds.). *Pädagogisches Lexikon,* Vol. 2. Gütersloh: Bertelsmann, cols. 1053-1055.

————. 1970a. *Die junge Generation. Jugend und Gesellschaft in der Bundesrepublik,* 3rd ed. Opladen: Leske.

————. 1971. ''Modernisierung' der Erziehung. Ansätze und Thesen zu einer Soziologie der Sozialisation.' In: FRANZ RONNEBERGER (ed.). *Sozialisation durch Massenkommunikation.* Stuttgart: Enke, pp. 1-20.

NELL-BREUNING, OSWALD VON. 1962. 'Sozialisierung.' In:

188   Bibliography

Staatslexikon, Vol. 7. Freiburg: Herder, cols. 295-303.

NESTLE, WERNER. 1975. 'Die Formulierung von Unterrichtsmodellen, Lehrplanungen und Arbeitsanweisungen.' In: KARL FREY (ed.). *Curriculum-Handbuch*, in 3 Vols. Munich: Piper, Vol. 2, pp. 170-178.

NEUGEBAUER, WILFRIED. 1980. 'Didaktische Modellsituationen.' In: HERBERT STACHOWIAK (ed.). *Modelle und Modelldenken im Unterricht. Anwendung der allgemeinen Modelltheorie auf die Unterrichtspraxis.* Bad Heilbrunn: Klinkhardt, pp. 50-73.

NICKLIS, WERNER S. 1967. *Kybernetik und Erziehungswissenschaft. Eine kritische Darstellung ihrer Beziehungen.* Bad Heilbrunn: Klinkhardt.

NIMKOFF, MEYER F. 1964. 'Socialization.' In: JULIUS GOULD and WILLIAM L. KOLB (eds.). *A Dictionary of the Social Sciences*. New York: Free Press, pp. 672-673.

NITSCH, HANS-JOACHIM. 1972. 'Ist 'Konflikt' der Schlüsselbegriff der politischen Bildung?' In: *Unterricht heute* 23, pp. 475-477.

NUNNER-WINKLER, GERTRUD and ROLFF, HANS-G. 1971. 'Theorie der Sozialisation.' In: THOMAS ELLWEIN /HANS-HERMANN GROOTHOFF/HANS RAUSCHENBERGER /HEINRICH ROTH (eds.). *Erziehungswissenschaftliches Handbuch*, Vol. 3. Berlin: Rembrandt, pp. 177-201.

NUTHALL, GRAHAM and SNOOK, IVAN. 1973. 'Contemporary Models of Teaching.' In: ROBERT M. W. TRAVERS (ed.). *Second Handbook of Research on Teaching.* Chicago: Rand McNally, pp. 47-76.

ODENBACH, KARL. 1974. *Lexikon der Schulpädagogik.* Braunschweig: Westermann.

OERTEL, FRITHJOF. 1977. 'Konflikt, Konflikterziehung.' In: *Wörterbuch der Pädagogik*, Vol. 2. Freiburg: Herder, pp. 181-183.

OEVERMANN, ULRICH. 1979. 'Sozialisationstheorie.' In: GÜNTHER LÜSCHEN (ed.). *Deutsche Soziologie seit 1945.* Opladen: Westdeutscher Verlag, pp. 143-168.

OPPENHEIMER, FRANZ. 1922. *System der Soziologie*, Vol. 1: *Allgemeine Soziologie, Erster Halbband: Grundlegung*. Jena: Gustav Fischer.

———. 1923. *System der Soziologie*, Vol. 1: *Allgemeine Soziologie, Zweiter Halbband: Der Soziale Prozess*. Jena: Gustav Fischer.

ORBAN, PETER. 1973. *Sozialisation. Grundlinien einer Theorie emanzipatorischer Sozialisation*. Frankfurt: Athenäum-Fischer.

Oxford English Dictionary, 2nd ed. 1989. Oxford: Clarendon.

Oxford Latin Dictionary. 1968. Oxford: Clarendon.

PARSONS, TALCOTT. 1951. *The Social System*. New York: Free Press.

———. 1964. *Social Structure and Personality*. Glencoe, IL: Free Press.

———, and BALES, ROBERT F. 1964. *Family, Socialization and Interaction Process*, 2nd ed. Glencoe, IL: Free Press.

PARTRIDGE, ERIC. 1966. *Origins. A Short Etymological Dictionary of Modern English*. London: Routledge & Kegan Paul.

PETERSEN, PETER. 1924. *Allgemeine Erziehungswissenschaft*. Berlin: de Gruyter.

PETTINGER, RUDOLF. 1974. 'Bedingungen und Zielsetzungen des Projekts 'Tagesmütter.' In: *Zeitschrift für Pädagogik* 20, pp. 913-927.

PFAUTZ, RUDOLF. 1974. "Konfliktfähigkeit' und 'Konfliktdidaktik' als Ziel und Mittel politischer Erziehung und Bildung in der Sekundarstufe II des Bildungssystems der BRD.' In: *Wissenschaftliche Zeitschrift der Pädagogischen Hochschule 'Karl Liebknecht' Potsdam* 18, pp. 615-636.

PITTIONI, VEIT. 1983. 'Modelle und Mathematik.' In: HERBERT STACHOWIAK (ed.). *Modell-Konstruktion der Wirklichkeit*. Munich: Fink, pp. 171-221.

PÖGGELER, FRANZ. 1964. *Der Mensch in Mündigkeit und Reife. Eine Anthropologie des Erwachsenen*. Paderborn: Schöningh.

POIRIER, FRANK E. (ed.). 1972. *Primate Socialization*. New

York: Random House.

————. 1977. 'Introduction.' In: SUZANNE CHEVALIER-SKOLNIKOFF and FRANK E. POIRIER (eds.). *Primate Bio-Social Development: Biological, Social, and Ecological Determinants.* New York: Garland, pp. 1-39.

POLANYI, MICHAEL. 1962. *Personal Knowledge,* 2nd ed. London: Routledge & Kegan Paul.

POPP, WALTER. 1970. 'Die Funktion von Modellen in der didaktischen Theorie.' In: GÜNTHER DOHMEN and FRIEDEMANN MAURER (eds.). *Unterrichtsforschung und didaktische Theorie.* Munich: Piper, pp. 49-60.

POPPER, KARL. 1964. 'Naturgesetze und theoretische Systeme.' In: HANS ALBERT (ed.). *Theorie und Realität.* Tübingen: Mohr.

POSCH, PETER. 1967. *Der Lehrermangel. Ausmaß und Möglichkeiten der Behebung.* Weinheim: Beltz.

PRIEBE, LONGIN. 1977. 'Sozialisation und Erziehung.' In: *Wörterbuch der Pädagogik,* Vol. 3. Freiburg: Herder, pp. 177-179.

RAUCH, EBERHARD and ANZINGER, WOLFGANG (eds.). 1973. *Wörterbuch Kritische Erziehung,* 4th ed. Starnberg: Raith.

RAUSCHENBERGER, HANS. 1975. 'Der Einfluß schulorganisatorischer Reformmodelle auf die Entwicklung von Curricula.' In: KARL FREY (ed.). *Curriculum-Handbuch,* in 3 Vols. Munich: Piper, Vol. 3, pp. 57-67.

REIN, WILHELM. 1895. 'Beispiel.' In: WILHELM REIN (ed.). *Encyklopädisches Handbuch der Pädagogik,* Vol. 1. Langensalza: Beyer, pp. 296-298.

Revised Medieval Latin Word-List. From British and Irish Sources. 1983. Edited by R.E. LATHAM. London: Oxford University Press.

RHONHEIMER, MARTIN. 1977. 'Sozialisation oder Erziehung? Die neue Bedrohung der Familie.' In: *Die Politische Meinung* 22, No. 175, pp. 39-58.

RICKERT, HEINRICH. 1922. *Die Philosophie des Lebens. Darstellung und Kritik der philosophischen Mode-*

strömungen unserer Zeit, 2nd ed. Tübingen: Mohr.

RITTIG, GISBERT. 1956. 'Sozialisierung: Theorie.' In: *Handwörterbuch der Sozialwissenschaften*, Vol. 9. Stuttgart: Gustav Fischer, pp. 455-464.

ROESSLER, WILHELM. 1976. 'Schichtenspezifische Sozialisation in der Weimarer Republik.' In: MANFRED HEINEMANN (ed.). *Sozialisation und Bildungswesen in der Weimarer Republik*. Stuttgart: Klett, pp. 17-38.

ROHRACHER, HUBERT. 1963. *Einführung in die Psychologie*, 8th ed. Vienna: Urban & Schwarzenberg.

RÖHRS, HERMANN. 1973. *Allgemeine Erziehungswissenschaft*, 3rd ed. Weinheim: Beltz.

ROLFF, HANS-GÜNTER. 1974. *Strategisches Lernen in der Gesamtschule. Gesellschaftliche Perspektiven der Schulreform*. Introduction by CARL-H. EVERS. Reinbek: Rowohlt.

RÖSSNER, LUTZ. 1973. *Theorie der Sozialarbeit*. Munich: Reinhardt.

———. 1977. *Erziehungs- und Sozialarbeitswissenschaft. Eine einführende Systemskizze*. Munich: Reinhardt.

ROTH, HEINRICH. 1967. *Erziehungswissenschaft, Erziehungsfeld und Lehrerbildung*. Hannover: Schroedel.

———. (ed.). 1969. *Begabung und Lernen. Ergebnisse und Folgerungen neuer Forschungen*. Stuttgart: Klett.

———. 1971. *Pädagogische Anthropologie*, Vol. 2: *Entwicklung und Erziehung. Grundlagen einer Entwicklungspädagogik*. Hannover: Schroedel.

ROTH, KARL-FRIEDRICH. 1970. *Möglichkeiten und Wege der Friedenserziehung. Theoretische und schulpraktische Überlegungen zur Konfliktpädagogik*. Sonderbeilage zu den Heften 12-15 der *Neuen Deutschen Schule* 22.

RUPRECHT, HORST/BECKMANN, HANS-KARL/CUBE, FELIX VON /SCHULZ, WOLFGANG. 1972. *Modelle grundlegender didaktischer Theorien*. Hannover: Schroedel.

RYLE, GILBERT. 1952. *The Concept of Mind*. London:

192   Bibliography

Hutchinson.

SACHER, HERMANN. 1931. 'Sozial.' In: *Staatslexikon*, Vol. 4. Freiburg: Herder, col. 1641.

SAILER, JOHANN MICHAEL. 1822. *Über Erziehung für Erzieher*, 3rd ed. (1962). Paderborn: Schöningh.

SALZMANN, CHRISTIAN. 1974. 'Die Bedeutung des Modellbegriffs in Unterrichtsforschung und Unterrichtsplanung.' In: LEO ROTH and GERHARD PETRAT (eds.). *Unterrichtsanalysen in der Diskussion*. Hannover: Schroedel, pp. 171-205.

———. 1975. 'Die Bedeutung der Modelltheorie für die Unterrichts-Planung unter besonderer Berücksichtigung hochschuldidaktischer Konsequenzen.' In: *Bildung und Erziehung* 28, pp. 258-279.

———, and KOHLBERG, WOLF-DIETER. 1983. 'Modellunterricht und Unterrichtsmodell.' In: *Zeitschrift für Pädagogik* 29, pp. 929-946.

SALZMANN, CHRISTIAN GOTTHILF. 1780. *Krebsbüchlein oder Anweisung zu einer unvernünftigen Erziehung der Kinder* (1948). Berlin: Volk und Wissen.

SCHAEFER, GERHARD/TROMMER, GERHARD/WENK, KLAUS (eds.). 1977. *Denken in Modellen*. Braunschweig: Westermann.

SCHALLER, KLAUS. 1970. 'Prozeß und Progreß einer Konflikterziehung.' In: *Lexikon der Pädagogik*. New Edition, Vol. 2. Freiburg: Herder, p. 474.

SCHIEDER, WOLFGANG. 1984. 'Sozialismus.' In: OTTO BRUNNER /WERNER CONZE/REINHART KOSELLECK (eds.). *Geschichtliche Grundbegriffe. Historisches Lexikon zur politisch-sozialen Sprache in Deutschland*, Vol. 5. Stuttgart: Klett-Cotta, pp. 923-996.

SCHILLER, HERMANN and LINDNER, GUSTAV ADOLF. 1906. 'Anschauungsunterricht.' In: JOSEPH LOOS (ed.). 1906 /08. *Enzyklopädisches Handbuch der Erziehungskunde*, in 2 Vols. Vienna: Pichler, Vol. 1, pp. 29-36.

SCHMIDT, WOLFGANG. 1980. 'Theorie und Modell.' In: *Zeitschrift für erziehungswissenschaftliche Forschung* 14, pp. 161-184.

SCHNEIDER, FRIEDRICH. 1953. *Einführung in die Erzie-*

hungswissenschaft, 2nd ed. Graz: Styria.

SCHNEIDER, KARL. 1978. 'Die Bedeutung 'didaktischer Modelle' in der Lehrerausbildung.' In: WERNER LOCH (ed.). *Modelle pädagogischen Verstehens*. Essen: Neue Deutsche Schule, pp. 141-160.

SCHULZ, WOLFGANG. 1980. *Unterrichtsplanung*. Munich: Urban & Schwarzenberg.

SCHÜRMANN, HANS WERNER. 1977. *Theoriebildung und Modellbildung*. Wiesbaden: Akademische Verlagsanstalt.

SCHWEIZER, HARRO. 1980. 'Modelldenken in Sprachwissenschaft und Sprachdidaktik.' In: HERBERT STACHOWIAK (ed.) *Modelle und Modelldenken im Unterricht. Anwendung der allgemeinen Modelltheorie auf die Unterrichtspraxis*. Bad Heilbrunn: Klinkhardt, pp. 144-160.

SEARS, ROBERT R./MACCOBY, ELEANOR E./LEVIN, HARRY. 1957. *Patterns of Child Rearing*. Evanston, IL: Row, Peterson.

———. 1977. 'Der Prozeß der Kindererziehung (child rearing).' In: HELMUT BONN and KURT ROSMANITH (eds.). *Eltern-Kind-Beziehung*. Darmstadt: Wissenschaftliche Buchgesellschaft, pp. 13-24.

SECORD, PAUL F. and BACKMAN, CARL W. 1974. *Social Psychology*, 2nd ed. New York: McGraw-Hill.

———, and SLAVITT, DAVID R. 1976. *Understanding Social Life. An Introduction to Social Psychology*. New York: McGraw-Hill.

SIMMEL, GEORG. 1909. 'The Problem of Sociology.' Translated by *Albion W. Small*. In: *American Journal of Sociology* 15, No. 3, pp. 289-320.

———. 1910. 'How is Society Possible?' Translated by ALBION W. SMALL. In: *American Journal of Sociology* 16, pp. 372-391.

———. 1950. *The Sociology of Georg Simmel*. Translated by KURT H. WOLFF. New York: Free Press.

———. 1955. *Conflict and the Web of Group Affiliations* (1908). Translated by KURT H. WOLFF. New York: Free Press.

———. 1958. *Soziologie. Untersuchungen über die Formen*

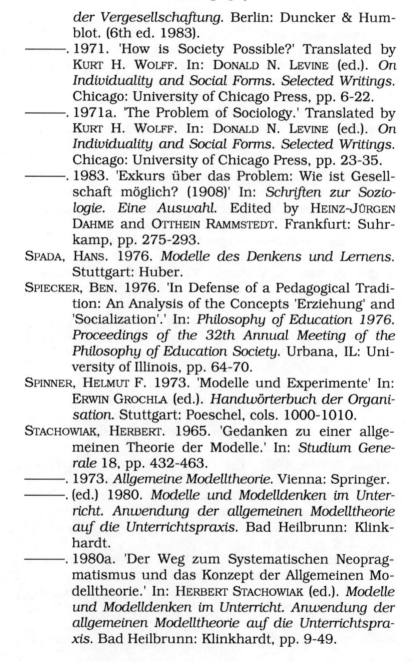

der *Vergesellschaftung*. Berlin: Duncker & Humblot. (6th ed. 1983).

———. 1971. 'How is Society Possible?' Translated by KURT H. WOLFF. In: DONALD N. LEVINE (ed.). *On Individuality and Social Forms. Selected Writings.* Chicago: University of Chicago Press, pp. 6-22.

———. 1971a. 'The Problem of Sociology.' Translated by KURT H. WOLFF. In: DONALD N. LEVINE (ed.). *On Individuality and Social Forms. Selected Writings.* Chicago: University of Chicago Press, pp. 23-35.

———. 1983. 'Exkurs über das Problem: Wie ist Gesellschaft möglich? (1908)' In: *Schriften zur Soziologie. Eine Auswahl.* Edited by HEINZ-JÜRGEN DAHME and OTTHEIN RAMMSTEDT. Frankfurt: Suhrkamp, pp. 275-293.

SPADA, HANS. 1976. *Modelle des Denkens und Lernens.* Stuttgart: Huber.

SPIECKER, BEN. 1976. 'In Defense of a Pedagogical Tradition: An Analysis of the Concepts 'Erziehung' and 'Socialization'.' In: *Philosophy of Education 1976. Proceedings of the 32th Annual Meeting of the Philosophy of Education Society.* Urbana, IL: University of Illinois, pp. 64-70.

SPINNER, HELMUT F. 1973. 'Modelle und Experimente' In: ERWIN GROCHLA (ed.). *Handwörterbuch der Organisation.* Stuttgart: Poeschel, cols. 1000-1010.

STACHOWIAK, HERBERT. 1965. 'Gedanken zu einer allgemeinen Theorie der Modelle.' In: *Studium Generale* 18, pp. 432-463.

———. 1973. *Allgemeine Modelltheorie.* Vienna: Springer.

———. (ed.) 1980. *Modelle und Modelldenken im Unterricht. Anwendung der allgemeinen Modelltheorie auf die Unterrichtspraxis.* Bad Heilbrunn: Klinkhardt.

———. 1980a. 'Der Weg zum Systematischen Neopragmatismus und das Konzept der Allgemeinen Modelltheorie.' In: HERBERT STACHOWIAK (ed.). *Modelle und Modelldenken im Unterricht. Anwendung der allgemeinen Modelltheorie auf die Unterrichtspraxis.* Bad Heilbrunn: Klinkhardt, pp. 9-49.

———. (ed.) 1983. *Modell-Konstruktion der Wirklichkeit.* Munich: Fink.

STEGMÜLLER, WOLFGANG. 1954. *Metaphysik, Wissenschaft, Skepsis.* Vienna: Humboldt.

———. 1969-74. *Probleme und Resultate der Wissenschaftstheorie und Analytischen Philosophie,* in 4 Vols. Berlin: Springer.

STEINBUCH, KARL. 1971. *Automat und Mensch. Auf dem Weg zu einer kybernetischen Anthropologie,* 4th ed. Heidelberg: Springer.

STEINER, ELIZABETH. 1978. *Logical and Conceptual Analytic Techniques for Educational Researchers.* Washington: University Press of America.

———. 1981. 'Logic of Education and of Educology: Dimensions of Philosophy of Education.' In: JAMES E. CHRISTENSEN (ed.). *Perspectives on Education as Educology.* Washington: University Press of America, pp. 87-99.

STEINER-MACCIA, ELIZABETH/MACCIA, GEORGE S./JEWETT, ROBERT E. (eds.). 1963. *Construction of Educational Theory Models.* Cooperative Research Project No. 1632, Columbus, OH: Ohio State University.

STIEGLITZ, HEINRICH. 1975. 'Sozialisierung als Erziehung zu sozialem Denken.' In: PANOS XOCHELLIS and HELMUT DEBL (eds.). *Denkmodelle für die Pädagogik.* Munich: Ehrenwirth, pp. 133-173.

———. 1976. 'Erziehung oder Sozialisation?' In: *Pädagogische Rundschau* 30, pp. 395-425.

STOFF, VIKTOR A. 1969. *Modellierung und Philosophie.* Berlin: Akademie.

STRAASS, GERHARD. 1963. *Modell und Erkenntnis. Zur erkenntnistheoretischen Bedeutung der Modellmethode in der Biologie.* Jena: Gustav Fischer.

STRAUBE, HARALD (ed.). 1966. *Modell eines neuen Gymnasiums. Eine Denkschrift des Schul- und Kulturreferats der Stadt Nürnberg.* Freiburg: Rombach.

STRZELEWICZ, WILLY. 1974. 'Erziehung und Sozialisation.' In: *Soziologie für die Schule,* 2nd ed. Freiburg: Herder, pp. 181-207.

SUPPES, PATRICK. 1969. 'A Comparison of the Meaning and

Uses of Models in Mathematics and the Empirical Sciences.' In: PATRICK SUPPES. *Studies in the Methodology and Foundations of Science.* Dordrecht: Reidel, pp. 10-23.

SÜSSMUTH, RITA. 1969. 'Erziehungsbedürftigkeit.' In: JOSEF SPECK and GERHARD WEHLE (eds.). *Handbuch pädagogischer Grundbegriffe*, Vol. 1. Munich: Kösel, pp. 405-424.

TACK, WERNER H. 1969. 'Mathematische Modelle in der Sozialpsychologie.' In: CARL F. GRAUMANN (ed.). *Sozialpsychologie (Handbuch der Psychologie)*, Vol. 7, I. Göttingen: Hogrefe, pp. 232-265.

TARSKI, ALFRED. 1971. *Undecidable Theories.* Amsterdam: North-Holland.

TAUSCH, REINHARD and TAUSCH, ANNE-MARIE. 1963. *Erziehungspsychologie. Psychologische Vorgänge in Erziehung und Unterricht.* Göttingen: Hogrefe, 8th ed. 1977.

THIEL, SIEGFRIED. 1976. 'Zum Problem der Vereinfachung und der Modellvorstellung bei Martin Wagenschein.' In: HUBERTUS HALBFAS/FRIEDEMANN MAURER /WALTER POPP (eds.). *In Modellen denken.* Stuttgart: Klett, pp. 22-31.

THOMAE, HANS. 1959. 'Entwicklungsbegriff und Entwicklungstheorie.' In: HANS THOMAE (ed.). *Entwicklungspsychologie (Handbuch der Psychologie*, Vol. 3). Göttingen: Hogrefe, pp. 3-20.

———. (ed.) 1965. *Allgemeine Psychologie. 2. Motivation (Handbuch der Psychologie*, Vol. 2). Göttingen: Hogrefe.

TOPITSCH, ERNST. 1960. 'Über Leerformeln.' In: ERNST TOPITSCH (ed.). *Probleme der Wissenschaftstheorie. Festschrift für Viktor Kraft.* Vienna: Springer, pp. 233-264.

ULICH, DIETER. 1976. 'Zur Methodik der Sozialisationsforschung.' In: KLAUS HURRELMANN (ed.). *Sozialisation und Lebenslauf: Empirie und Methodik sozialwissenschaftlicher Persönlichkeitsforschung.* Reinbek: Rowohlt, pp. 53-67.

———. 1986. 'Kriterien psychologischer Entwicklungsbegriffe.' In: *Zeitschrift für Sozialisationsforschung und Erziehungssoziologie* 6, pp. 5-27.

ULICH, KLAUS. 1981. 'Sozialisation.' In: HANS SCHIEFELE and ANDREAS KRAPP (eds.). *Handlexikon zur Pädagogischen Psychologie*. Munich: Ehrenwirth, pp. 343-349.

Ullstein Lexikon der deutschen Sprache. 1969. Frankfurt: Ullstein.

UPLEGGER, FRITZ. 1976. 'Zur Kritik der Konfliktdidaktik.' In: *Gegenwartskunde* 25, pp. 317-326.

USCHMANN, GEORG. 1968. 'Die Naturgeschichte des biologischen Modells.' In: JOACHIM-HERMANN SCHARF and GÜNTER BRUNS (eds.). *Biologische Modelle*. Bericht über die Jahresversammlung der Deutschen Akademie der Naturforscher Leopoldina vom 19. bis 22. Oktober 1967 in Halle (Saale) (Nova acta Leopoldina, Neue Folge), Nr. 184. Leipzig: Barth, pp. 43-64.

WARTOFSKY, MARX W. 1979. *Models. Representation and the Scientific Understanding*. Dordrecht: Reidel.

WEBER, MAX. 1972. *Wirtschaft und Gesellschaft*, 5th ed. Tübingen: Mohr.

———. 1978. *Economy and Society: An Outline of Interpretive Sociology*, Vol. I. Edited by GUENTHER ROTH and CLAUS WITTICH. Berkeley/Los Angeles/London: University of California Press.

Webster's New World Dictionary of American English, Third College Edition. 1988. New York: Simon and Schuster.

WEIL, MARSHA and JOYCE, BRUCE. 1978. *Social Models of Teaching. Expanding Your Teaching Repertoire*. Englewood Cliffs, NJ: Prentice-Hall.

WEISS, CARL. 1929. *Pädagogische Soziologie*. Leipzig: Klinkhardt.

WENDLER, GERNOT. 1965. 'Über einige Modelle in der Biologie.' In: *Studium Generale* 18, pp. 284-290.

WENIGER, ERICH. 1960. *Didaktik als Bildungslehre*. Weinheim: Beltz.

WENTWORTH, WILLIAM M. 1980. *Context and Understanding: An Inquiry into Socialization Theory*. New

198   Bibliography

York: Elsevier North Holland.

WIELAND, CHRISTOPH MARTIN. 1984. *Sämtliche Werke*, Vol. 29: *Vermischte Aufsätze*. 1797. Leipzig: Göschen. Reprint Hamburg: Greno.

WILHELM, THEODOR. 1969. *Theorie der Schule*, 2nd ed. Stuttgart: Metzler.

WILLMANN, OTTO. 1930. *The Science of Education in its Sociological and Historical Aspects*, in 2 Vols. Translated by FELIX M. KIRSCH. Latrobe, PA: Archabbey.

————. 1957. *Didaktik als Bildungslehre*, 6th ed. Vienna: Herder.

————. 1980. 'Allgemeine Pädagogik. Die Erziehung als Erneuerung der Gesellschaft' (1875). In: *Sämtliche Werke*, Vol. 4. Aalen: Scientia, pp. 1-145.

WILSHIRE, BRUCE. 1977. 'Role Playing and Identity: The Limits of the Theatrical Metaphor.' In: *Cultural Hermeneutics* 4, pp. 199-207.

WINKELMANN, WOLFGANG/HOLLÄNDER, ANTJE/SCHMERKOTTE, HANS/ SCHMALOHR, EMIL. 1977. *Kognitive Entwicklung und Förderung von Kindergarten- und Vorklassenkindern. Bericht über eine längsschnittliche Vergleichsuntersuchung zum Modellversuch des Landes Nordrhein-Westfalen*. Kronberg/Taunus: Scriptor.

WOLF, ANTONIUS. 1970. 'Konflikterziehung.' In: *Lexikon der Pädagogik*. New Edition, Vol. 2. Freiburg: Herder, pp. 473-474.

————. 1976. 'Konflikterziehung.' In: *Wörterbuch der Vorschulerziehung*. Freiburg: Herder, pp. 177-179.

WOLLENWEBER, HORST (ed.). 1981. *Modelle sozialpädagogischer Theoriebildung*. Paderborn: Schöningh.

WURZBACHER, GERHARD. 1963. 'Sozialisation—Enkulturation—Personalisation.' In: GERHARD WURZBACHER (ed.). *Der Mensch als soziales und personales Wesen*. Stuttgart: Enke, pp. 1-34.

ZIGLER, EDWARD. 1977. 'Socialization: An Overview.' In: BENJAMIN B. WOLMAN (ed.). *International Encyclopedia of Psychiatry, Psychology, Psychoanalysis, and Neurology*, Vol. 10. New York: Van Nostrand

Reinhold, pp. 304-309.

————, and CHILD, IRVIN L. 1969. 'Socialization.' In: GARDNER LINDZEY and ELLIOT ARONSON (eds.). *The Handbook of Social Psychology*, 2nd ed., Vol. 3. Reading, MA: Addison-Wesley, pp. 450-589.

————, and CHILD, IRVIN L. (eds.). 1973. *Socialization and Personality Development*. Reading, MA: Addison-Wesley.

ZILLER, TUISKON. 1876. *Vorlesungen über Allgemeine Pädagogik*. Leipzig: Matthes.

ZIMMERMANN, WALDEMAR. 1948. 'Das 'Soziale' im geschichtlichen Sinn- und Begriffswandel.' In: LUDWIG H. GECK *et al.* (eds.). *Studien zur Soziologie. Festgabe für Leopold von Wiese*, Vol. 1. Mainz: Internationaler Universum Verlag, pp. 173-191.

Name Index

Subject Index

About the Author

WOLFGANG BREZINKA is Professor and Director of the Department of Educational Science at the University of Konstanz in Germany. The author of 11 books on education, his works have been translated from German into eight foreign languages. His English publications include *Philosophy of Educational Knowledge* (1992), *Basic Concepts of Educational Science* (1994), and *Belief, Morals, and Education* (1994).